SPACE
NUMBER CRUNCH

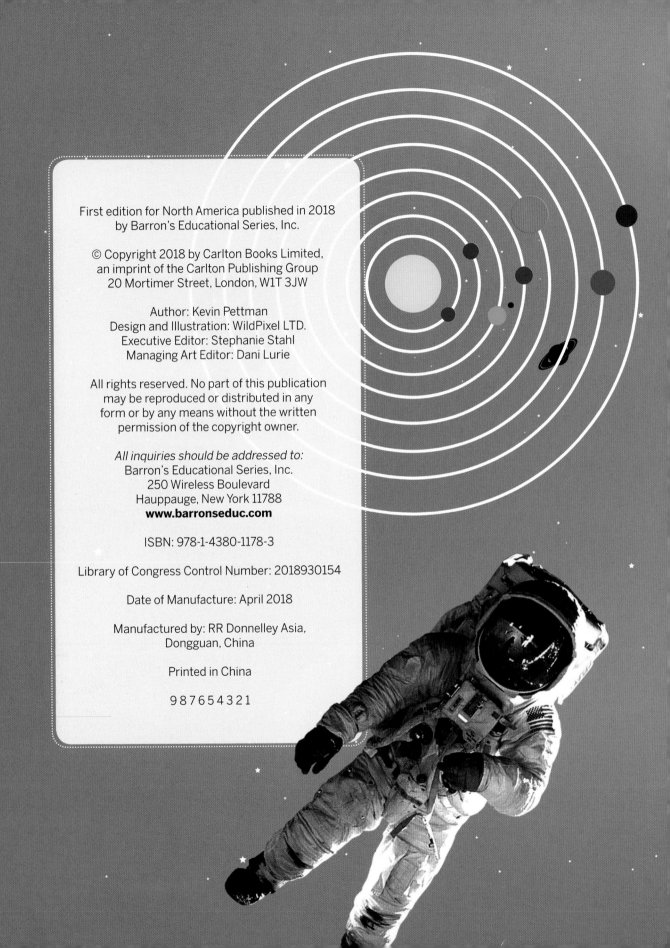

First edition for North America published in 2018
by Barron's Educational Series, Inc.

© Copyright 2018 by Carlton Books Limited,
an imprint of the Carlton Publishing Group
20 Mortimer Street, London, W1T 3JW

Author: Kevin Pettman
Design and Illustration: WildPixel LTD.
Executive Editor: Stephanie Stahl
Managing Art Editor: Dani Lurie

All inquiries should be addressed to:
Barron's Educational Series, Inc.
250 Wireless Boulevard
Hauppauge, New York 11788
www.barronseduc.com

ISBN: 978-1-4380-1178-3

Library of Congress Control Number: 2018930154

Date of Manufacture: April 2018

Manufactured by: RR Donnelley Asia,
Dongguan, China

Printed in China

9 8 7 6 5 4 3 2 1

SPACE
NUMBER CRUNCH

THE FIGURES, FACTS, AND SPACE STATS YOU NEED TO KNOW

KEVIN PETTMAN

BARRON'S

CONTENTS

SPECTACULAR SOLAR SYSTEM

Our Sun and the planets that move around it, including moons, asteroids, and comets, are called the solar system. Take a speedy spaceflight to discover some stunning stats and facts!

Venus is only the **SECOND** planet from the Sun but it has the hottest surface temperature. Its thick atmosphere traps heat, which can soar to **880°F (471°C)**.

The distance between Mars and Earth changes hugely because they orbit at different rates. Mars can be between **34 and 249 million mi (54.6 and 401 million km)** away.

There are **8** planets in our solar system. They all orbit (move around) the Sun at different speeds. Mercury is the closest to the Sun and is between **29 million mi (47 million km)** and **43 million mi (70 million km)** from it.

Mercury Venus   Earth   Mars

Jupiter

Earth has **1** Moon, which is an average of **238,855 mi (384,400 km)** from the planet. There are hundreds of moons in our solar system – Jupiter has **53** known moons and possibly **16** more!

Our planet, Earth, is the **THIRD** from the Sun. Earth is the biggest of the **4** rocky inner planets, which include Mercury, Venus, and Mars.

ALL PLANETS (WIDTH)

1. Jupiter	88,846 mi	(142,984 km)
2. Saturn	74,897 mi	(120,536 km)
3. Uranus	31,763 mi	(51,118 km)
4. Neptune	30,775 mi	(49,528 km)
5. Earth	7,926 mi	(12,756 km)
6. Venus	7,521 mi	(12,104 km)
7. Mars	4,220 mi	(6,792 km)
8. Mercury	3,032 mi	(4,879 km)

The **4** giant planets (Jupiter, Saturn, Uranus, and Neptune) are called gas giants. They don't have solid surfaces but at least three have a solid, rocky core (center). They are freezing cold and temperatures can be lower than **-328°F (-200°C)**.

Uranus is tilted at an angle of **98 DEGREES**, by far the most of any planet, and almost spins on its side.

Jupiter is so vast that more than **1,300** Earths could fit inside it.

Saturn

Uranus

Neptune

Saturn is known for its amazing ring system. There are **7** main rings, extending about **175,226 mi (282,000 km)** from Saturn.

Neptune is about **2.78 billion mi (4.5 billion km)** from the Sun. Because it's so distant, it takes over **4 HOURS** for sunlight to reach Neptune.

Our solar system exists in a galaxy called the Milky Way. It's thought there are between **100 BILLION** and **400 BILLION** stars in the Milky Way.

GET READY FOR A BIG BANG

The universe, which includes all planets, stars, animals, living things, and even time, began to be created **BILLIONS** of years ago by an explosion called the Big Bang.

The temperature at the start was **BILLIONS** of degrees Fahrenheit (billions of degrees Celsius).

Most experts think the Big Bang happened about **13.8 BILLION YEARS** ago when everything that became the current universe appeared in a tiny space and instantly expanded.

At its very beginning, the universe expanded incredibly quickly. This is known as the Inflation Era and the universe could have doubled in size more than **100** times in much less than **1 SECOND**.

It took **1 MILLIONTH OF A SECOND** for the universe to cool down so that particles of energy could become the beginnings of atoms.

Within the first few minutes of the Big Bang, the temperature could still have been about **1 BILLION DEGREES**.

It took about **300,000 YEARS** for the temperature to drop to around **5,432°F (3,000°C)**. During this phase, hydrogen and helium atoms formed neutral atoms, and then light energy (photons) was able to pass through space.

Cosmic Microwave Background (CMB) is radiation from the Big Bang. It formed about **380,000 YEARS** after the event and was discovered in **1964** using a radio antenna.

Between **200** and **400 MILLION YEARS** after the Big Bang, enough gas had been collected to begin the formation of stars and galaxies. This was called reionization and happened for up to **1 BILLION YEARS**.

The Sun began forming from gases and dust **4.6 BILLION YEARS** into the universe's life.

The **8** planets formed shortly afterward from the material left over from the formation of our solar system.

After a massive asteroid struck Earth, asteroid and Earth material came together because of gravity to form our Moon. This was about **4.5 BILLION YEARS** ago, and **9.3 BILLION YEARS** after the Big Bang.

About **3.85 BILLION YEARS** ago, bacteria started to develop on Earth. This was the earliest form of life.

HELLO SUNSHINE!

The Sun is the biggest object in the solar system and provides life-giving energy to Earth. It's a true super star!

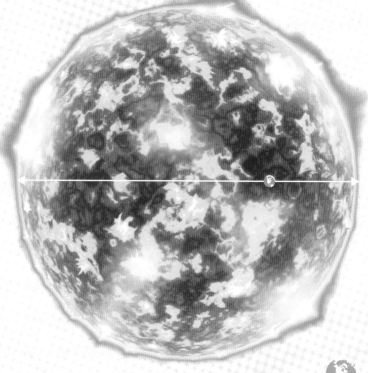

The Sun is over **864,938 mi (1,390,000 km)** wide. It's **333,000** times heavier than Earth.

About **1,300,000** Earths could fit inside the Sun.

x 1,300,000 EARTHS

The Sun

8 MIN

Earth

Sunlight takes **8 MINUTES** to reach Earth from the Sun. It travels at nearly **186,000 mph (300,000 km/h)**.

99.8%

Of all the mass in the entire solar system, the Sun accounts for **99.8 PERCENT** of it.

8.9%

0.1%

91%

The Sun is a massive ball of gas. **91 PERCENT** hydrogen atoms, **8.9 PERCENT** helium atoms, and **0.1 PERCENT** of other chemicals.

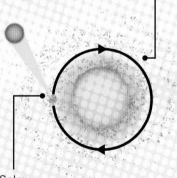

67

As well as hydrogen and helium, there are at least **67** other chemical elements inside the Sun.

6 LAYERS MAKE UP THE SUN . . .

1. Core
2. Radiative zone
3. Convective zone
4. Photosphere
5. Chromosphere
6. Corona

230 MILLION years orbit

Solar System

Everything in the solar system orbits the Sun, but the solar system orbits the center of the Milky Way galaxy. The solar system takes about **230 MILLION YEARS** to orbit the Milky Way.

5 BILLION YEARS

Scientists think the Sun will burn for about **10 BILLION YEARS**. It has been burning for **5 BILLION YEARS** so it will be providing energy and light for another **5 BILLION YEARS**.

WARNING

UV Protection

NEVER LOOK DIRECTLY AT THE SUN! IT WILL DAMAGE YOUR EYES.

SUN-THING SPECTACULAR

From solar cycles to surface gravity and energy to eclipses, the Sun produces all sorts of spectacular stats.

The Sun provides Earth with **3** main types of energy, in the form of waves: infrared radiation, visible light, and ultraviolet light (UV). UV waves have the most energy and can give people a tan, but too much can be harmful.

1. Infrared radiation — the Sun gives off about **50 PERCENT** of its total energy as infrared radiation. It is invisible heat.

2. Visible light — this is the energy from the Sun that we experience as sunlight.

3. Ultraviolet light — is very powerful and can even reach Earth through clouds.

Imagine a bar of ice **1.8 mi (3 km)** wide and approx. **1 mi (1.5 km)** thick extending all the way from Earth to the Sun. The Sun would have enough energy to melt it in just **1 SECOND**!

1 SECOND

The Helios 2 spacecraft is the machine that's been closest to the Sun, but it still only came within **27 million mi (43.5 million km)** of it in **1976**.

Helios 2 reached a record top speed of **43.63 mi per second (70.22 km per second)**.

27 million mi (43.5 million km)

Sun

Helios 2

Because the Sun is not solid but a ball of gas, it does not all rotate at the same rate. An area near the Sun's equator makes a full rotation every **25 EARTH DAYS**, but an area at the poles can take up to **38 DAYS**.

Equator

38 DAYS

25 DAYS

38 DAYS

NUMBER CRUNCH
The temperature of the Sun is **59 million °F (15 million °C)** at the core, dropping to **9,932 °F (5,500°C)** at the nominal surface (photosphere).

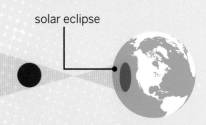

solar eclipse

Experts have worked out that between **2000 BCE** and the year **3000** there will be **11,898** eclipses of the Sun. A solar eclipse happens in daytime when the Moon moves in front of the Sun.

65 mph (105 km/h)

If a car could drive non-stop in a straight line at **65 mph (105 km/h)** from Earth to the Sun, it would take about **163 YEARS** and **120 DAYS** to reach the Sun.

11 YEARS

Roughly every **11 YEARS**, the solar cycle of the Sun changes. This causes storms and disruptions in the Sun's photosphere, chromosphere, and corona. The activity can even damage satellites and affect power supplies on Earth.

Sunspots are whirlpools near the photosphere that suck hot gas into the Sun. They are about **2,732°F (1,500°C)** cooler than the photosphere and can be **49,712 mi (80,000 km)** across – **6** times the width of Earth.

Earth   Sun

The Sun's surface gravity is **28** times stronger than gravity on Earth. This means if you weigh **110 lb (50 kg)** on Earth, you'll be about **3,086 lb (1,400 kg)** on the Sun!

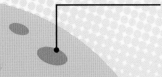

MERCURY IN THE SPOTLIGHT

Mercury is the closest planet to the Sun and is blasted by solar radiation. But because it rotates slowly, much of the planet can be freezing cold while the rest is boiling hot!

As it's so close to the Sun (between **29** and **43 million mi (47** and **70 million km)** Mercury is extremely hot. It can reach **806°F (430°C)** on the surface.

The thin atmosphere doesn't protect Mercury from sunlight, but at night the temperature can drop to **-292°F (-180°C)** because the atmosphere doesn't keep heat in.

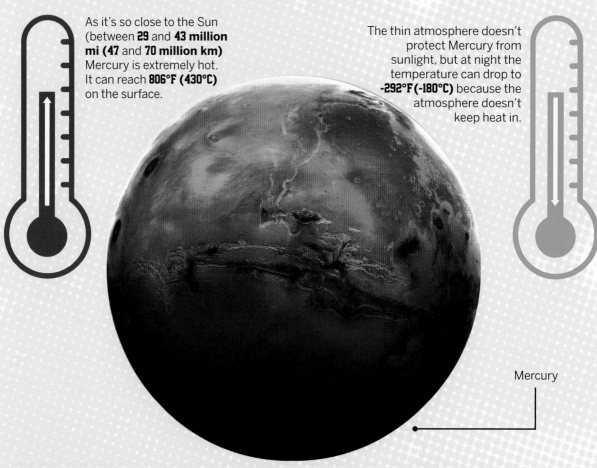

Mercury

13 times each century, Mercury can be seen passing in front of the Sun. This is called a transit.

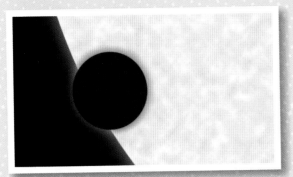

Transits only occur in early May and early November. The next one will be in **2019**.

88 DAYS

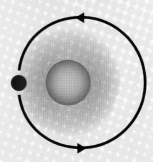

It orbits the Sun in just **88 DAYS**, which is the quickest orbit of all planets in the solar system.

If you stood on Mercury at the point nearest the Sun, the Sun would look more than **3** times bigger than it does on Earth.

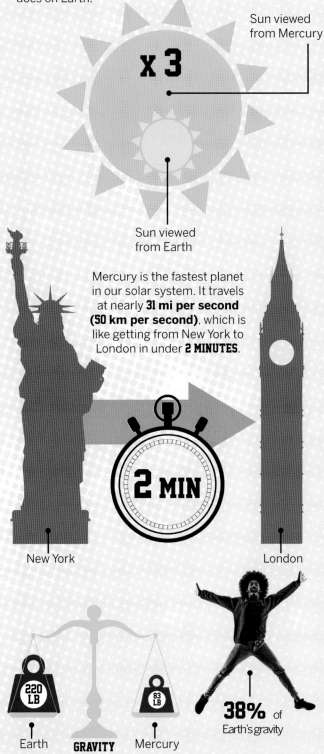

Sun viewed from Mercury

x 3

Sun viewed from Earth

Mercury is the fastest planet in our solar system. It travels at nearly **31 mi per second (50 km per second)**, which is like getting from New York to London in under **2 MINUTES**.

2 MIN

New York

London

GRAVITY

Earth

220 LB

Mercury

83 LB

38% of Earth's gravity

Gravity on Mercury is only **38 PERCENT** of Earth's gravity, so you would weigh much less on Mercury than you do on Earth, and you could easily bounce around on the surface a bit like astronauts did on the Moon.

MISSIONS TO MERCURY

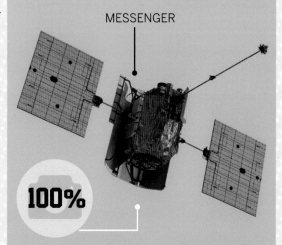

MESSENGER

100%

Between **2011** and **2013**, the MESSENGER spacecraft photographed **100 PERCENT** of Mercury's surface. The first spacecraft to explore Mercury, in **1974–1975**, Mariner 10, imaged just **45 PERCENT**.

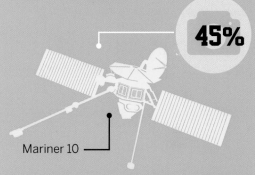

45%

Mariner 10

MESSENGER crashed into Mercury in **2015** at a speed of about **8,700 mph (14,000 km/h)** after completing **4,105** orbits.

1 DAY on Mercury is the same as **59 DAYS** on Earth. The planet travels fast but spins very slowly on its axis.

MERCURY	EARTH
DAY 1	DAY 59

MAGNIFICENT MERCURY

Let's stick around on Mercury to discover a stash of mindblowing numbers all about this tiny planet.

Mercury was heavily struck by meteoroids and asteroids in its early formation around **4 BILLION YEARS** ago, leaving tons of craters on the surface.

Caloris Basin

The force of the asteroid impact that created the Caloris Basin could have equaled **1 TRILLION 1-MEGATON** hydrogen bombs.

The largest known crater is the Caloris Basin, which is about **963 mi (1,550 km)** wide. The soccer field at Wembley Stadium would fit across it, end to end, **14,750** times.

1 TRILLION

Hydrogen bomb

x **14,750**

peak

Craters larger than about **9 miles (15 km)** often have a peak, or peaks, in the center that look like a mountain.

Experts think the presence of carbon in Mercury's outer crust helps to make it the darkest planet in the solar system. Mercury reflects just **11 PERCENT** of sunlight.

11%

Mercury

Mercury has the least tilt (lean) of any planet. It's almost upright, with a tilt of about just **0.027 DEGREES**.

Mercury

Venus

Earth

Mars

Jupiter

Saturn

Uranus

Neptune

MESSENGER

But sunlight can be up to **10** times brighter on the planet. The MESSENGER spacecraft had a special heat-resistant sunshade.

Mercury has no atmosphere so it can't support life as we know it.

Although it's very small, Mercury is very dense, the **2ND** densest planet after Earth. It's made of **60 PERCENT** metal and **40 PERCENT** rock.

Mercury's core probably takes up **85 PERCENT** of its diameter.

NUMBER CRUNCH
Mercury is tiny and would fit inside Earth **18** times.

HOT STUFF

Here you'll uncover so much red-hot information about the sweltering surface of Venus, you may need oven gloves just to turn the page!

Molten lead

Venus is the hottest planet in the solar system, with temperatures always between **863°F (462°C)** and **878°F (470°C)**.

878°F (470°C)

Conditions on Venus are hot enough to melt the metal lead and **8** times hotter than the hottest places on Earth.

Venus

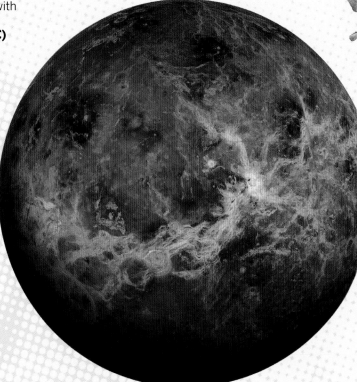

Venus has around **900** named craters on its surface, which is low compared to other planets and objects.

Because Venus has a thick atmosphere reflecting a lot of light, it is the **3RD** brightest object in the sky after the Sun and Moon.

24 MILLION MI

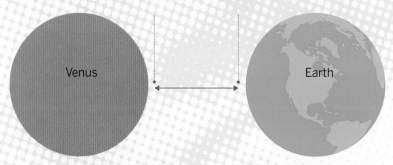

Venus

Earth

At their closest orbits, Venus is **24 million mi (38 million km)** away from Earth, which is closer than any other planet.

Venus is usually visible for less than **3 HOURS** a day. In the evening, it can appear in the west of the sky, or in the morning it can be seen in the east before the Sun rises.

The atmosphere of Venus is **96.5 PERCENT** carbon dioxide, which causes a greenhouse effect and stops heat from escaping.

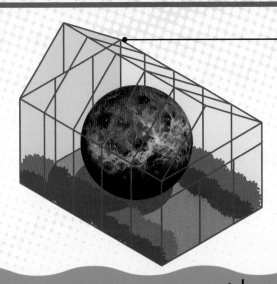

932°F (500°C)

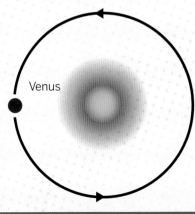

The atmosphere on Venus is **92** times heavier than Earth's. That's the same pressure as the water pressing down on a submarine **0.6 mi (1 km)** below the surface of the ocean.

Venus tilts at just **3 DEGREES**. This means it doesn't have seasons like Earth and hardly any difference in temperature between the equator and the poles.

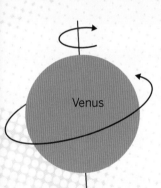

Venus

Venus

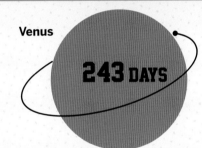

243 DAYS

The planet completes 1 rotation on its axis in **243 EARTH DAYS**. That's the slowest of all **8** planets.

There are more than **1,600** large volcanoes and maybe **A MILLION** small ones on Venus, more than any other planet.

Venus orbits the Sun in only **225 EARTH DAYS**, which is the second quickest after Mercury.

Venus

The smallest craters are **1.2 mi (2 km)** wide and the largest are **174 mi (280 km)** wide. Small meteoroids burn up in the planet's powerful atmosphere before reaching the surface.

Experts think Venus was resurfaced by volcanic activity between **300** and **500 MILLION YEARS** ago.

VENUS FACT TRAP

With its toxic gases and baking heat, humans would only survive a few seconds on Venus. You'll spend much longer taking in these top facts and stats!

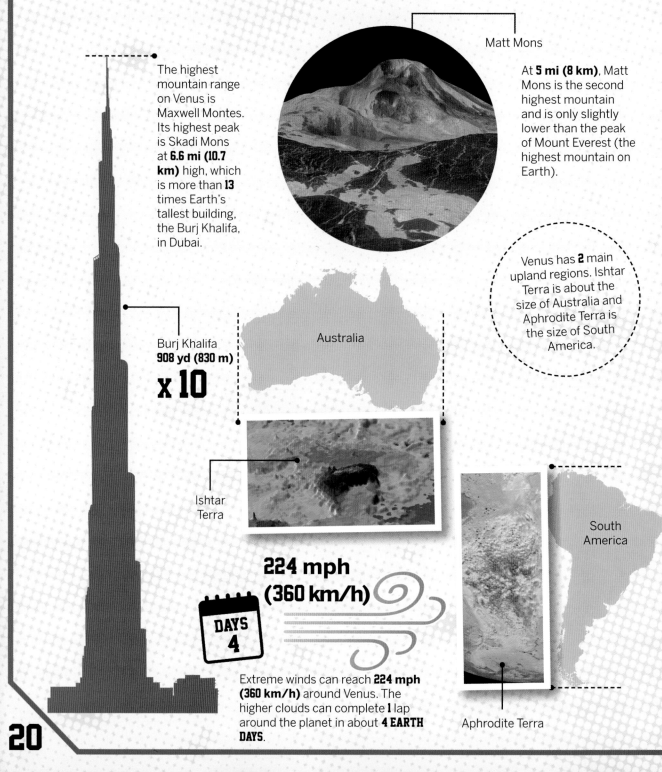

Matt Mons

At **5 mi (8 km)**, Matt Mons is the second highest mountain and is only slightly lower than the peak of Mount Everest (the highest mountain on Earth).

The highest mountain range on Venus is Maxwell Montes. Its highest peak is Skadi Mons at **6.6 mi (10.7 km)** high, which is more than **13** times Earth's tallest building, the Burj Khalifa, in Dubai.

Venus has **2** main upland regions. Ishtar Terra is about the size of Australia and Aphrodite Terra is the size of South America.

Burj Khalifa
908 yd (830 m)

x 10

Australia

Ishtar Terra

South America

224 mph (360 km/h)

DAYS 4

Extreme winds can reach **224 mph (360 km/h)** around Venus. The higher clouds can complete **1** lap around the planet in about **4 EARTH DAYS**.

Aphrodite Terra

Venus' diameter is **7,521 mi (12,104 km)**.

Earth's diameter is **7,926 mi (12,756 km)**.

Venus is often called Earth's twin planet. It's only **405 mi (652 km)** smaller in diameter and has **81.5 PERCENT** of the mass of Earth.

Venera 7

25 spacecrafts have successfully approached Venus, and **9** of those have landed. The **1ST** to land and send data back to Earth was **VENERA 7**, launched by the USSR in **1970**.

Venus

Venus has an apparent magnitude of about **-4.7** at its brightest. This describes how easy it is to be seen from Earth. Objects that are easier to see have lower magnitudes (the Sun has a magnitude of **-27**).

77%

About **77 PERCENT** of sunlight that reaches Venus is reflected back into space by its thick acidic clouds.

Venus is extremely hot and the only place where temperatures are similar to those on Earth is about **31 mi (50 km)** above the surface in Venus' atmosphere.

Venus has phases, just like the Moon. These can only be seen through a telescope, and were first seen by Galileo in **1610**.

21

HOME SWEET HOME

No planet is quite like Earth. Its atmosphere, temperature, and water supply are essential for human, animal, and plant life as we know it. We could not survive on any other planet of the solar system.

Earth

Every **4 YEARS**, **1 DAY** is added to the calendar, making that year **366 DAYS** long. This is because Earth doesn't orbit at exactly **365** days.

DAY
365̶6̶

SPEED LIMIT
66,622 mph
(107,218 km/h)

Earth moves around the Sun at a speed of **66,622 mph (107,218 km/h)**. That's about **1,531** times faster than the motorway speed limit in Britain **(70 mph [112 km/h])**.

Earth spins on its axis once every **24 HOURS** and completes an orbit of the Sun in **365 DAYS**.

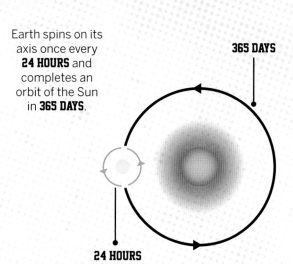

365 DAYS

24 HOURS

Earth is tilted at an angle of **23.5 DEGREES**. The part of its surface that gets direct sunlight is warmer and brighter than the part that has less direct sunlight at the same time.

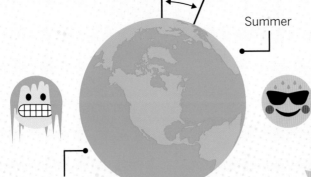

Summer

Winter

This tilt causes summer and winter seasons. In countries north of the equator, like Britain and Canada, summer is from about May to August, but the same period is winter in countries that are south of the equator, such as Australia.

The continent of Antarctica, around the south pole, is the coldest place on Earth. Its average inland temperature is **-30°F (-34.4°C)** and the lowest ever recorded was **-129°F (-89.4°C)**.

6 MONTHS

In the winter, Antarctica has **6 MONTHS** of continual darkness with **6 MONTHS** of continual daylight in the summer.

6 MONTHS

The highest recorded air temperature on the ground was **134°F (56.7°C)** in Death Valley, California. The average temperature on Earth is **59°F (15°C)**.

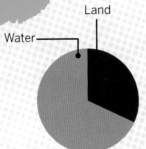

Land

Water

About **70 PERCENT** of Earth's surface is covered by water. The oceans and seas contain **97 PERCENT** of the water on Earth.

32%

The largest ocean is the Pacific, which takes up about **32 PERCENT** of the Earth's surface.

Earth's atmosphere has **5** layers.

1. Troposphere. From the ground and extends **5 to 9 mi (8 to 14 km)** high.
2. Stratosphere. Rises to about **31 mi (50 km)** and includes the ozone layer.
3. Mesosphere. Approximately **53 mi (85 km)** high with temperatures of **-148°F (-100°C)**.
4. Thermosphere. Over **373 mi (600 km)** thick and reaches more than **3,632°F (2,000°C)**.
5. Exosphere. Outer layer reaches to **6,214 mi (10,000 km)** above Earth.

The atmosphere is **78 PERCENT** nitrogen, **21 PERCENT** oxygen, and **1 PERCENT** argon, carbon dioxide, and other gases.

1   2   3   4   5

UNEARTHING MORE FACTS

With over **9 MILLION** different forms of life, there's a lot happening on—and below—the surface of our astonishing home planet.

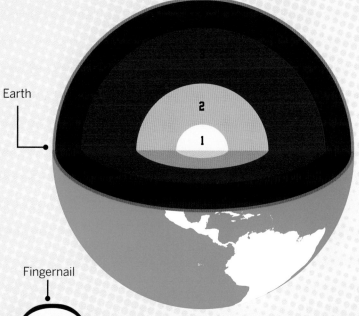

Earth

There are **4** main layers inside Earth.

1. Inner core. Solid iron and nickel at about **9,752°F (5,400°C)**.

2. Outer core. Molten metal, cooler at around **7,232°F to 9,032°F (4,000°C to 5,000°C)**.

3. Mantle. Made of semi-liquid rocks, ranging from **7,232°F to 932°F (4,000°C to 500°C)** nearer the crust.

4. Crust. At the surface, it's the temperature of Earth's air, which varies across the planet. Around the equator, the temperature can be **104°F (40°C)** or higher.

Fingernail

The crust and upper-mantle of the Earth are divided into huge plates—they are constantly moving. Some move at the same rate that human fingernails grow— over **1.18 in (3 cm)** a year.

1 AU

Earth is an average distance of **92.9 million mi (149.6 million km)** from the Sun. This distance is **1** astronomical unit (AU) and is an easy way to compare distances in space.

Earth is not named after an ancient Greek or Roman god. The other **7** planets are.

9 MILLION

Of the **9 MILLION** different forms of life on Earth, about **75 PERCENT** of these live on land.

Some experts reckon there could be **1.3 BILLION** insects for every person on the planet.

Moon

Sun

gravitational pull

When Earth spins on its axis, it wobbles slightly, partly because of the gravitational pull of the Sun and Moon.

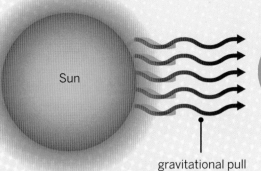

Studying rocks tells us that life on Earth could have begun **4 BILLION YEARS** ago in the form of micro-organisms and simple bacteria.

WHEN DID THEY FIRST APPEAR?

Arthropods (spiders, insects, and crustaceans) **542 MILLION YEARS** ago.

Fish **530 MILLION YEARS** ago.

Plants **470 MILLION YEARS** ago.

Forests **385 MILLION YEARS** ago.

Mammals **210 MILLION YEARS** ago.

Homo sapiens (modern humans) **200,000 YEARS** ago. Humans have been on Earth for just **0.004 PERCENT** of its history.

Blue whale

The largest animal on Earth today, and the largest ever known (including dinosaurs), is the blue whale. It can weigh over **396,830 lb (180,000 km)** and be **108 ft (33 m)** long.

That's nearly as long as **3** London buses.

London bus

Earth's average sea level has risen by around **7.87 in (20 cm)** in the past **100 YEARS**, a result of global warming. Global warming is caused by gases from things like cars and burning coal that are trapping heat in the atmosphere.

MISSION TO MARS

Humans have been exploring Mars for over **50 YEARS**, but the famous Red Planet is still mysterious and mesmerizing.

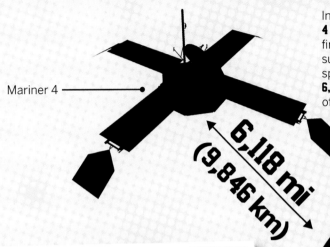

Mariner 4

In **1965**, America's Mariner **4** spacecraft took the first ever pictures of the surface of Mars from space. It came within **6,118 mi (9,846 km)** of the planet.

6,118 mi (9,846 km)

Mars

Earth

Mars

The world waited until **1976** for a spacecraft to land successfully on Mars and send images to Earth. Viking **1** took **11 MONTHS** to reach the planet after travelling over **434,959,834 mi (700,000,000 km)**.

Mars is just over **50 PERCENT** the size of Earth, with a diameter of **4,220 mi (6,792 km)**.

In August **2003**, Mars was **34,646,419 mi (55,758,006 km)** from Earth—the nearest the two had been for nearly **60,000 YEARS**.

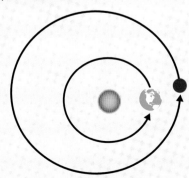

Mars has a thin atmosphere, which doesn't trap heat, and is much farther from the Sun than Earth. Its average temperature is a freezing **-81.4°F (-63°F)**.

-193°F (-125°C)

68°F (20°C)

Temperatures range from a frightfully cold **-193°F (-125°C)** to a warm **68°F (20°C)** depending on where you are on the planet.

If a grown-up stood on the equator at midday, the temperature could feel like **75.2°F (24°C)** at your feet but only **32°F (0°C)** by your head.

CO₂

The atmosphere of Mars is mainly carbon dioxide (**95.3 PERCENT**). The surface pressure is just **1 PERCENT** of Earth's and the iron-rich red dust is why Mars is often called the Red Planet.

New York

Mars has some of the largest dust storms known. These can range from small dust storms to **1,243 mi (2,000 km)** wide storms—the distance between New York and Miami.

Miami

Its atmosphere has less than **0.2 PERCENT** oxygen, which means that humans and life as we know it could not exist on the surface of Mars.

Mars' Olympus Mons is the largest volcano in the solar system, at more than **15.5 mi (25 km)** high. It has gentle slopes and is **20** times wider than its height.

The volcano is **77** times the height of the Eiffel Tower in Paris.

x 77

MARVELOUS MARS

With evidence of water ice on the planet, Mars could one day be a stopping-off point for human spaceflights. But remember, it takes **9 MONTHS** to reach it from Earth!

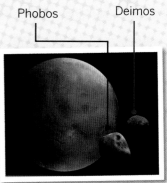

Phobos   Deimos

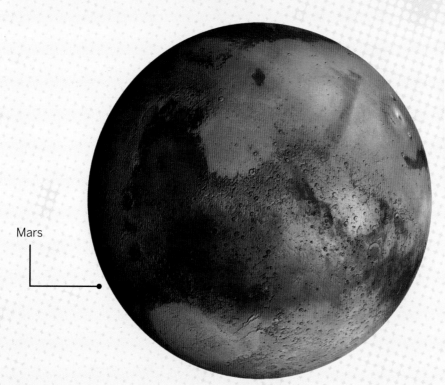

Mars

Mars has **2** small moons, called Phobos and Deimos, that are shaped a bit like potatoes and are respectively **7.5 mi (12 km)** and **13.7 mi (22 km)** across.

24 HOURS AND 37 MINUTES

One day on Mars is only slightly longer than on Earth. A day (the time it takes Mars to spin on its axis) is **24 HOURS** and **37 MINUTES**.

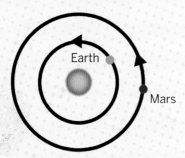

Earth

Mars

But a year (the time Mars takes to orbit the Sun) is nearly twice as long as Earth's at **687 DAYS**.

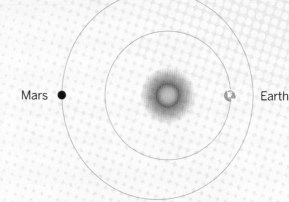

Mars

Earth

For about **2 WEEKS** every **2 YEARS**, Earth and Mars can't see each other because the Sun is directly between the planets. This is called solar conjunction.

Until about **3.7 BILLION YEARS** ago, Mars was wet and quite warm. In **2015**, NASA found evidence of liquid water flowing downhill on the surface.

Scientists predict that the water-ice caps at the poles are an average of **1.8 mi (3 km)** thick. If these were melted, they would cover the surface of Mars with over **16.4 ft (5 m)** of water.

Valles Marineris is a huge canyon on the surface of Mars. It covers **14 PERCENT** of the distance around the planet and is wider than the entire United States.

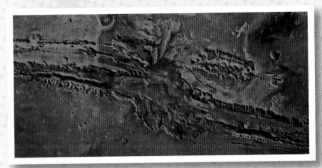

It's **1,864-mi (3,000-km)**-long and **5-mi (8-km)**-deep in places. It is a crack probably created when Mars cooled billions of years ago.

A rover called Opportunity landed on Mars in **2004**. By October **2017** it had covered **28 mi (45 km)**, as it explored the surface, examining its rocks and searching for signs of life.

Opportunity

Shortly after arriving, Opportunity discovered the mineral hematite in rocks. This mineral often forms in water.

Hematite in rocks

Spirit

An identical rover, called Spirit, landed at the same time but became stuck in soft soil in **2009** after covering just **4.8 mi (7.73 km)** of Mars' surface.

The planet has only **38 PERCENT** of Earth's gravity. That means an object weighing **220 lb (100 kg)** on Earth would be just **84 lb (38 kg)** on Mars.

220 LB

84 LB

Earth

Mars

9 MONTHS

With current technology, it would take **7–9 MONTHS** to travel to Mars from Earth. A spacecraft would then have to wait 3 or **4 MONTHS** as the **2** planets need to be in the right places, before a **9-MONTH** return trip. There is only a launch opportunity every **26** months.

THE KING OF PLANETS

Named after the king of ancient Roman gods, Jupiter's a massive gas giant with an even bigger story to tell. Read on to discover some gigantic chunks of information!

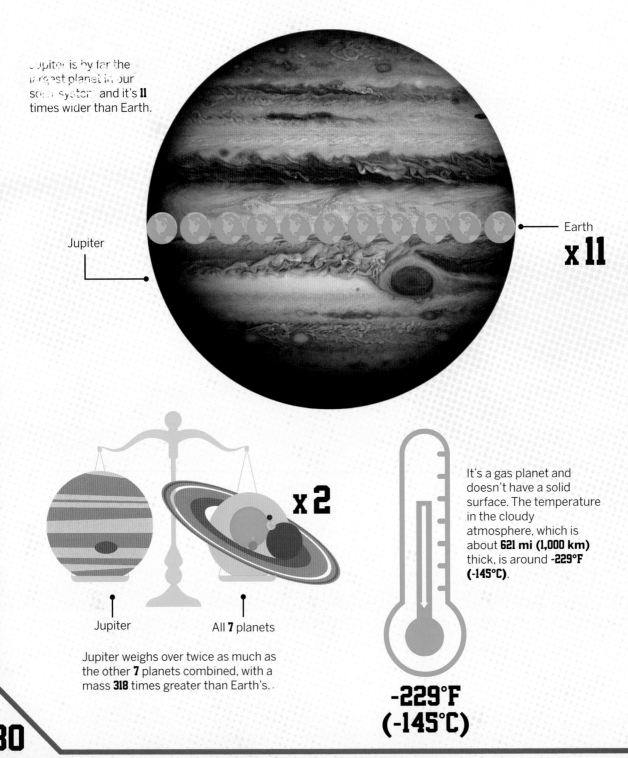

Jupiter is by far the largest planet in our solar system and it's **11** times wider than Earth.

Jupiter

Earth
x 11

x 2

Jupiter

All **7** planets

Jupiter weighs over twice as much as the other **7** planets combined, with a mass **318** times greater than Earth's. .

It's a gas planet and doesn't have a solid surface. The temperature in the cloudy atmosphere, which is about **621 mi (1,000 km)** thick, is around **-229°F (-145°C)**.

-229°F (-145°C)

10.2%   89.8%

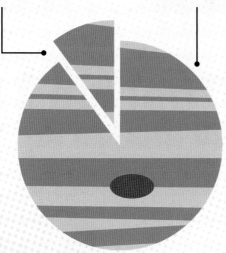

With **89.8 PERCENT** hydrogen and **10.2 PERCENT** helium in its atmosphere, Jupiter is similar to a star. If it had grown **80** times bigger, it would have become a star.

Jupiter probably has a solid, rocky core where temperatures could be **43,232°F (24,000°C)**, which is hotter than the Sun's surface.

43,232°F (24,000°C)

moons **x 69**

Jupiter is the planet with the most moons in our solar system. It has **69** moons in total.

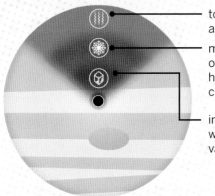

The pressure at the center of Jupiter is like being squashed by the force of **130,000** cars stacked on top of you. The same pressure at the center of Earth is about **10,000** cars.

x 130,000

A distinctive swirling cloud can be seen on the surface. Called the Great Red Spot, it was first identified in **1694** and then again in **1830**. It might be **1.3** times as wide as Earth.

Jupiter is colorful with pretty bands and stripes. It has **3** cloud gas layers, covering about **43 mi (70 km)**.

top cloud of ammonia and ice

middle cloud of ammonium hydrosulphide crystals

inner layer of water ice and vapor

384 mph (618 km/h)

Jupiter is a very windy planet. Around the equator these winds can reach **384 mph (618 km/h)**. The most intense hurricanes recorded on Earth only peak at around **186 mph (300 km/h)**.

A storm cloud called the Little Red Spot, nearly the width of Earth, was formed by **3** white-colored storms that were seen merging together in **1998** and **2000**.

GIANT JUPITER

Here are even more mega-sized facts and stats about the biggest planet in our solar system. Get ready for some giant-sized surprises...

483 million mi
(778 million km)

Jupiter is the **5TH** planet from the Sun and is just over **5** times further away from it than Earth is, at an average distance of **483 million mi (778 million km)**.

43 MINS

Sun

Jupiter

When sunlight leaves the Sun, it takes **43 MINUTES** to reach the planet.

In **1979**, scientists were surprised to discover that Jupiter has a ring system. There are **2** thicker rings and **2** very faint outer rings.

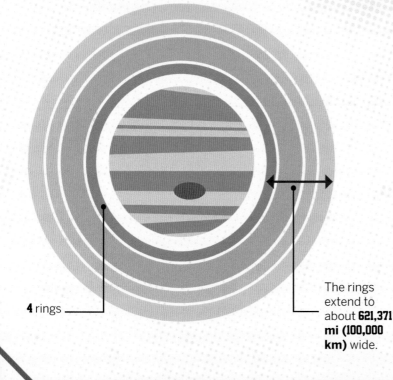

4 rings

The rings extend to about **621,371 mi (100,000 km)** wide.

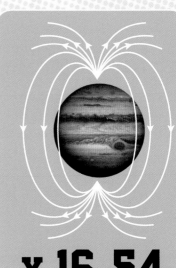

x 16-54

At **16–54** times greater than Earth, Jupiter has the most powerful magnetic field in the solar system, produced by the movement of a thick layer of liquid hydrogen that creates electricity.

1,864,114 mi
(3 million km)

x 21

The magnetosphere, which is the region that a planet's magnetic force can act on, extends to **1,864,114 mi (3 million km)** into space. That's **21** times longer than Jupiter's huge diameter.

Jupiter rotates (spins) faster than any other planet at about **26,719 mph (43,000 km/h)**. It creates an extremely strong magnetic field.

26,719 mph
(43,000 km/h)

It's thought that Jupiter could have an enormous ocean of liquid hydrogen that's about **12,427 mi (20,000 km)** deep. Earth's deepest ocean, the Pacific, is just **6.8 mi (11 km)** deep at most.

EARTH	JUPITER
DAY 1	10 HRS

One day on Jupiter is **10 HOURS** long, which is the shortest in the solar system. But its years are very long—**1 YEAR** on Jupiter is equal to nearly **12 YEARS** on Earth.

Not only does Jupiter have violent storms, but it also has incredible lightning strikes that are **HUNDREDS** of times brighter than on Earth.

Juno

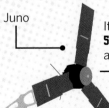

It took NASA's Juno space probe **5 YEARS** to reach Jupiter's orbit, after launching in 2011.

5 YEARS

Juno covered about **1.7 billion mi (2.8 billion km)** on the journey, which is the same as **70,000** trips around Earth's equator.

x 10 MILLION

Some of Jupiter's lightning is the same as **10 MILLION 100 WATT** light bulbs.

LORD OF THE RINGS

With its stunning ring system, Saturn is one of the most easily recognized objects in the night sky through a telescope. But this giant planet has many more fascinating features.

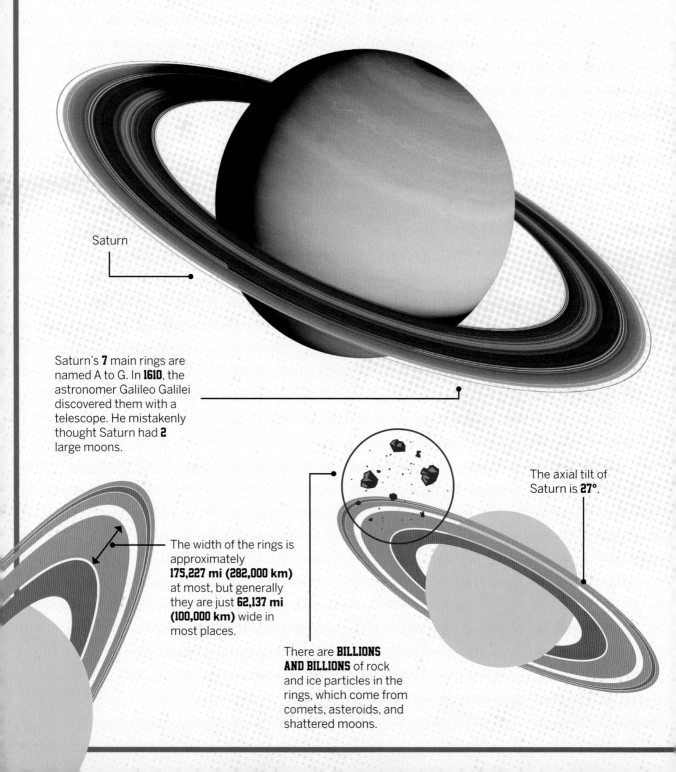

Saturn

Saturn's **7** main rings are named A to G. In **1610**, the astronomer Galileo Galilei discovered them with a telescope. He mistakenly thought Saturn had **2** large moons.

The width of the rings is approximately **175,227 mi (282,000 km)** at most, but generally they are just **62,137 mi (100,000 km)** wide in most places.

The axial tilt of Saturn is **27°**.

There are **BILLIONS AND BILLIONS** of rock and ice particles in the rings, which come from comets, asteroids, and shattered moons.

Every **14** to **15 YEARS**, the thin rings look as if they disappear when viewed from Earth. They are "edge on" and very thin when seen from our planet, due to Saturn's orbit.

The next time Saturn will be edge on to Earth will be in **2025**.

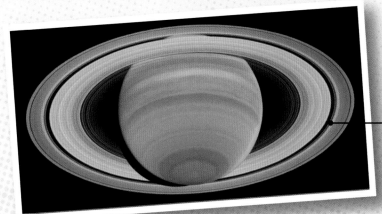

The rings are close together, with the largest gap being between rings B and A and measuring **2,920 mi (4,700 km)**. This gap is the Cassini Division.

Cassini Division

Saturn, at an average distance from Earth of **888.6 million mi (1.43 billion km)**, is the furthest planet that can be seen from ours without a telescope or binoculars.

The distance from Earth ranges from **745.6 million mi (1.2 billion km)** to **1.06 billion mi (1.7 billion km)** depending on orbits.

The temperature can be as low as **-288.4°F (-178°C)**.

-288.4°F (-178°C)

x 90

On average, an area on Earth would receive **90** times more sunlight than the same spot on Saturn.

x 62

There could be as many as **62** moons orbiting Saturn.

79 MIN

After it has left the Sun, sunlight takes **79 MINUTES** to reach the planet. Sunlight only takes about **8 MINUTES** to reach Earth.

STUNNING SATURN

Check out all these spectacular findings to become a super-brainy Saturn expert!

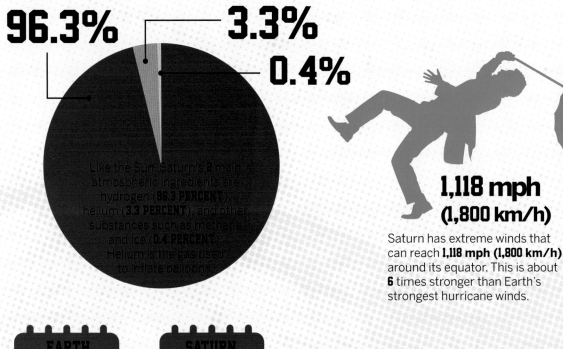

96.3%   **3.3%**

0.4%

Like the Sun, Saturn's 2 main atmospheric ingredients are hydrogen (**96.3 PERCENT**), helium (**3.3 PERCENT**), and other substances such as methane and ice (**0.4 PERCENT**). Helium is the gas used to inflate balloons.

1,118 mph (1,800 km/h)

Saturn has extreme winds that can reach **1,118 mph (1,800 km/h)** around its equator. This is about **6** times stronger than Earth's strongest hurricane winds.

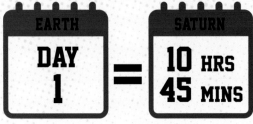

EARTH   **DAY 1**   **=**   **SATURN**   **10 HRS 45 MINS**

The huge planet spins very fast on its axis, with **1** day lasting an average of **10 HOURS** and **45 MINUTES**.

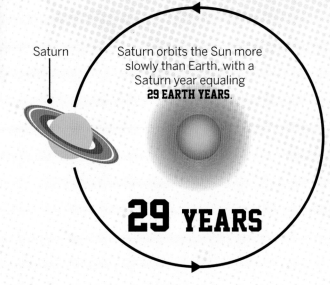

Saturn

Saturn orbits the Sun more slowly than Earth, with a Saturn year equaling **29 EARTH YEARS**.

29 YEARS

A strange **6**-sided cloud shape sits above Saturn's north pole. It's about **19,884 mi (32,000 km)** wide, with winds blowing at over **199 mph (320 km/h)**.

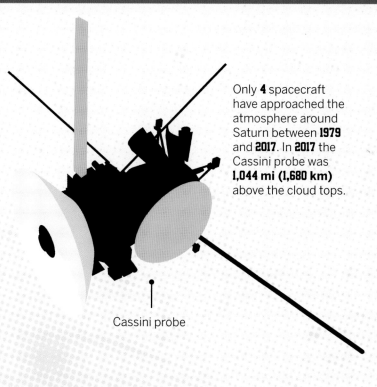

Only **4** spacecraft have approached the atmosphere around Saturn between **1979** and **2017**. In **2017** the Cassini probe was **1,044 mi (1,680 km)** above the cloud tops.

Cassini probe

Tyrannosaurus rex

Saturn's rings were once thought to have formed when dinosaurs still roamed Earth, a few **MILLION YEARS** ago, but most experts now believe they were created early on in the planet's **4.5-BILLION-YEAR** history.

Saturn is over **9** times wider than Earth, but because it's a gas giant it's less dense. If there was a bathtub big enough and filled with water, Saturn would float in it because it's less dense than water!

Saturn is the **6TH** planet from the Sun. Its closest planet can be Jupiter, at **407 million mi (655 million km)** away, but this can increase to **13.7 billion mi (2.21 billion km)** because the planets are always moving in their orbits.

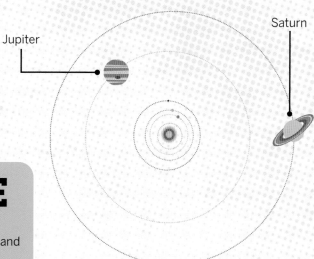

Jupiter

Saturn

MASS ÷ VOLUME

Density is the mass of an object divided by its volume. Mass is how much "stuff" is in an object and volume is how much space an object takes up.

YOUR ULTIMATE URANUS GUIDE

The distant planet Uranus is the seventh from the Sun and third biggest in our solar system. It's cold and hostile, but don't be frightened to explore these spectacular stats...

Uranus

EARTH
1 YEAR

=

URANUS
84 YEARS

Uranus takes a very long time to orbit the Sun and a year on the planet is equal to **84** Earth years – a human would have a maximum of **1** birthday there!

Uranus can experience temperatures as low as **-371.2°F (-224°C)**.

**-371.2°F
(-224°C)**

x 64

Uranus is **4** times wider than Earth and nearly **64** Earths would fit inside the massive ice giant.

97.77°

21 YEARS

21 YEARS

Because Uranus is tilted at **97.77 DEGREES**, its poles are pointed directly at the Sun at times. One pole has **21 YEARS** of constant sunshine while the other has **21 YEARS** of constant darkness. Each has **2** periods of **21 YEARS** of twilight.

2 HRS 40 MINS

Sun

Uranus

Sunlight takes **2 HOURS 40 MINUTES** to reach the planet after it has left the Sun. Sunlight passes through its methane-rich atmosphere and this gas absorbs the red part of the light, leaving Uranus with a blue-green color.

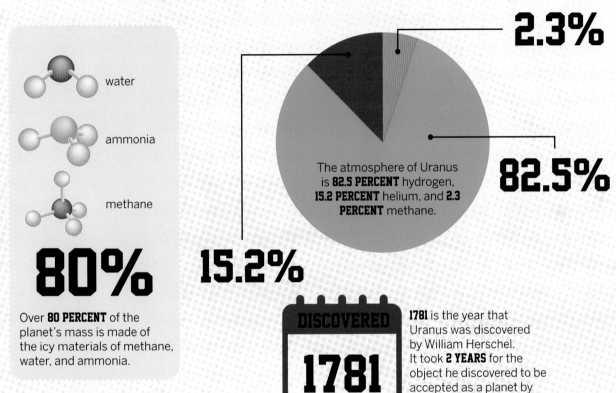

water

ammonia

methane

2.3%

The atmosphere of Uranus is **82.5 PERCENT** hydrogen, **15.2 PERCENT** helium, and **2.3 PERCENT** methane.

82.5%

15.2%

80%

Over **80 PERCENT** of the planet's mass is made of the icy materials of methane, water, and ammonia.

DISCOVERED

1781

1781 is the year that Uranus was discovered by William Herschel. It took **2 YEARS** for the object he discovered to be accepted as a planet by other astronomers.

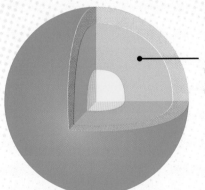

mantle

X 1,000,000

The pressure in the mantle within Uranus is more than **1 MILLION** times Earth's atmospheric pressure. Chemicals that would normally be liquids or gases can turn into solids.

559 mph (900 km/h)

The swirling atmosphere makes Uranus a very windy planet. Its winds can reach **559 mph (900 km/h)** and at the equator, they blow west to east, which is opposite to the way the planet spins.

UNBELIEVABLE URANUS

Uranus is the only planet named after a Greek god, rather than a Roman one. Uranus has fascinating numbers, too!

Uranus has **13** known rings, which weren't discovered until **1977**. They are very faint and need powerful telescopes to be seen from Earth.

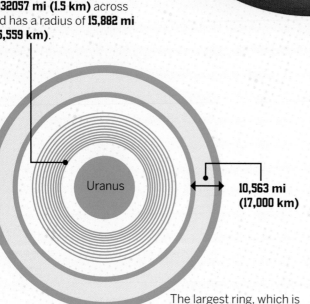

Uranus

The smallest ring is only **0.932057 mi (1.5 km)** across and has a radius of **15,882 mi (25,559 km)**.

Uranus

10,563 mi (17,000 km)

The largest ring, which is part of the **2** large outer rings, is **60,708 mi (97,700 km)** in radius and **10,563-mi (17,000-km)**-wide.

Because Uranus spins quite fast—a day lasts for **17 HOURS** and **14 MINUTES**—it bulges around its equator. It makes the planet look like a squashed ball!

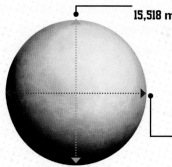

15,518 mi (24,973 km)

Its radius from pole to pole (top to bottom) is **15,518 mi (24,973 km)** but its equatorial radius (distance around the middle) is **15,882 mi (25,559 km)**—that's a difference of **364 mi (586 km)**.

15,882 mi (25,559 km)

x 27

Uranus has **27** moons that we know of and may have more that haven't yet been discovered.

Earth's Moon   Titania

Uranus's largest moon, which is nearly **994 mi (1,600 km)** in diameter, is called Titania. Earth's very own moon is more than twice as wide.

It took **161 YEARS** to discover the first **5** moons, between **1787** and **1948**.

CCCCC

1787–1948

In **1986** NASA's Voyager 2 spacecraft discovered **10** more moons all at once.

Uranus and Earth have similar gravity. Objects would weigh only slightly less there than they do on Earth.

The first recorded sighting of Uranus was in **1690**. It was called **34** Tauri and was thought to be a star.

Voyager

When William Herschel discovered Uranus in **1781**, he wanted to call it Georgium Sidus (the Georgian planet) after England's King George III.

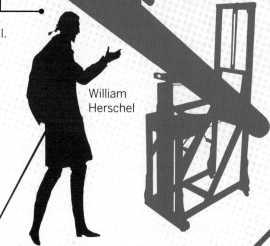

William Herschel

Voyager **2** was the first spacecraft to enter the orbit of Uranus. After traveling for nearly **9 YEARS**, in 1986 it came within **50,642 mi (81,500 km)** of the planet.

9 YEARS

Voyager **2**   Uranus

A PLANET FAR, FAR AWAY...

Neptune is between **2.7 and 2.9 billion mi (4.3 and 4.7 billion km)** away from Earth. Let's zoom to the outer edge of the solar system to take a closer look at this distant and mysterious planet!

Of the **8** planets, Neptune is the only one that needs a telescope to see it. The others are all visible, at times, with the naked eye.

Great Dark Spot

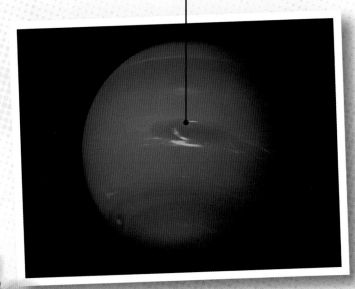

A huge storm, called the Great Dark Spot, was larger than Earth and was detected on Neptune in **1989**. It moved at about **746 mph (1,200 km/h)**.

5 YEARS later, images from the Hubble Space Telescope showed that the Great Dark Spot had disappeared.

But in **2016** a new Great Dark Spot was seen by NASA's Hubble Space Telescope.

Hubble Space Telescope

1,243 mph (2,000 km/h)

The winds on Neptune can reach nearly **1,243 mph (2,000 km/h)** and are the strongest winds we know of in the solar system.

They are about **6** times faster than Earth's most extreme winds.

165 YEARS

Because it's the furthest planet from the Sun, it takes Neptune **165 EARTH YEARS** to completely orbit the Sun, which is more than any other planet.

2.8 billion mi (4.5 billion km)

Neptune is about **30** times further away from the Sun than Earth is, at about **2.8 billion mi (4.5 billion km)**.

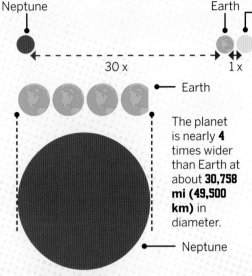

Neptune   Earth   Sun

30 x   1 x

Earth

The planet is nearly **4** times wider than Earth at about **30,758 mi (49,500 km)** in diameter.

Neptune

30,758 mi (49,500 km)

19%

1%

80%

Neptune's atmosphere only has between **1–2 PERCENT** of a gas called methane but even at that low level, methane still gives it its bright blue colour. About **80 PERCENT** of it is hydrogen and around **19 PERCENT** is helium.

In the **1800s**, it was the first planet to be located through working out clever mathematical equations rather than through regular sightings by telescope.

Neptune's largest moon, Triton, is probably one of the coldest places in the solar system with a temperature of **-391°F (-235°C)**. Scientists know of **13** confirmed moons around Neptune and **1** newly discovered in 2013.

Experts reckon that in **10 to 100 MILLION YEARS**, Neptune's gravity could cause Triton to break up before they collide, and it will form a ring system around the planet.

GET IN TUNE WITH NEPTUNE

Cast your eyes over these far-out facts from our solar system's most far-out planet. Put the light on though, because it's dark and gloomy there!

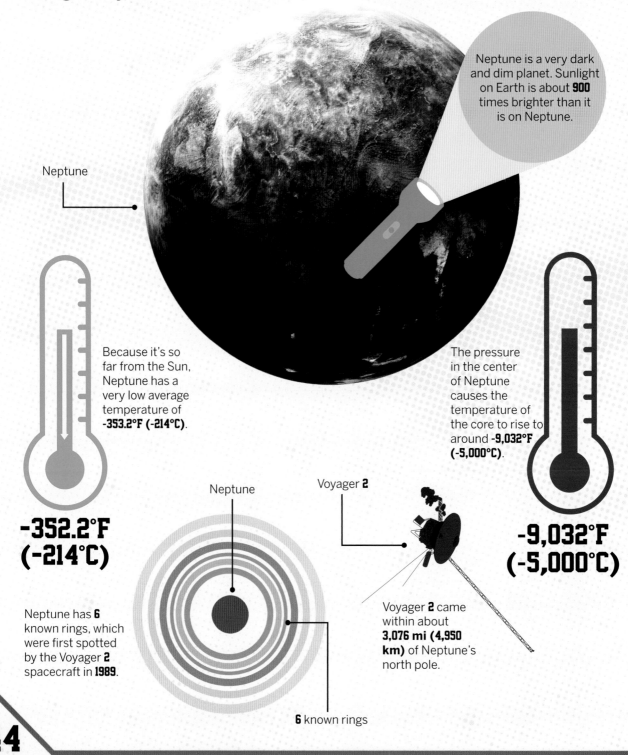

Neptune is a very dark and dim planet. Sunlight on Earth is about **900** times brighter than it is on Neptune.

Neptune

Because it's so far from the Sun, Neptune has a very low average temperature of **-353.2°F (-214°C)**.

The pressure in the center of Neptune causes the temperature of the core to rise to around **-9,032°F (-5,000°C)**.

-352.2°F (-214°C)

Neptune has **6** known rings, which were first spotted by the Voyager **2** spacecraft in **1989**.

Neptune

Voyager **2**

Voyager **2** came within about **3,076 mi (4,950 km)** of Neptune's north pole.

-9,032°F (-5,000°C)

6 known rings

The outer ring is **38,146 mi (63,000 km)** away from the center of Neptune.

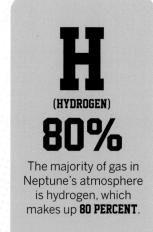

Jupiter

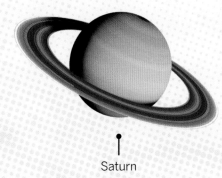

Saturn

Uranus

Neptune

Neptune is the smallest of the **4** gas giants, behind Jupiter, Saturn, and Uranus, but is the densest of all **4** of these planets.

28.3°

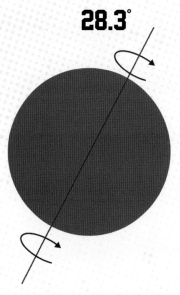

The planet tilts at an angle of **28.3°**. This means that its **4** seasons can last for over **40 YEARS** each.

SEASONS

40 YEARS

Because it is the furthest planet from the Sun, it takes Neptune **165 EARTH YEARS** to completely orbit the Sun, which is more than any other planet.

165 YEARS

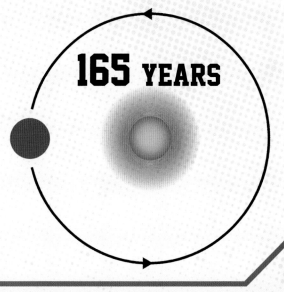

LITTLE PLANET PLUTO

Much smaller than the **8** regular planets, Pluto has been known to humans for less than **100 YEARS**. In that time we've discovered quite a lot about it.

Pluto

Pluto was discovered in **1930** and was classed as the solar system's **9TH** planet for **76 YEARS**. In **2006** that changed and it was officially called a dwarf planet.

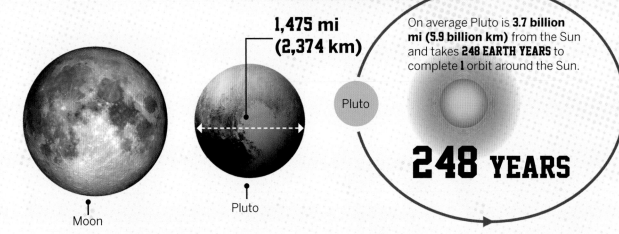

1,475 mi (2,374 km)

Moon

Pluto

Pluto

On average Pluto is **3.7 billion mi (5.9 billion km)** from the Sun and takes **248 EARTH YEARS** to complete **1** orbit around the Sun.

248 YEARS

Its diameter is **1,475 mi (2,374 km)**, which is only about **2/3** the size of our Moon.

Pluto moves around the Sun in an oval orbit. Because of this, between **1979** and **1999** it was actually nearer to the Sun than Neptune was.

The next time Pluto is at its furthest point from the Sun will be in the year **2112**.

There are **5** moons that orbit Pluto. The largest, called Charon, is only **12,204 mi (19,640 km)** away from Pluto.

Pluto

Charon

In comparison, the average distance between Earth and our Moon is **238,855 mi (384,400 km)**.

Earth

Moon

Pluto is located in a distant region beyond Neptune called the Kuiper Belt. The Kuiper Belt could have more than **100,000** icy objects larger than **62 mi (100 km)**.

Scientists don't know exactly how cold Pluto is but estimate the surface temperature to be as low as **-396°F (-238°C)**.

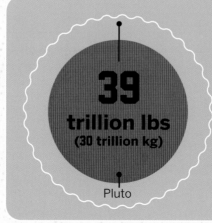

39 trillion lbs (30 trillion kg)

Pluto

Pluto's surface is probably covered with frozen nitrogen. The ice sublimates (changes directly from a solid to a gas) and forms a very small atmosphere. The planet only has **39 trillion lbs (30 trillion kg)** of atmosphere whereas Earth has **11 quintillion lbs (5 quintillion kg)**, which is **150,000** times as much.

-396°F
(-238°C)

DWARF PLANETS UNDER THE MICROSCOPE

They may be little and difficult to study because they're so far from Earth, but dwarf planets like Ceres, Eris, and Makemake are still worth a closer look...

The year **2006** was very important for dwarf planets. This was when the International Astronomical Union (IAU) defined the rules for what makes an object a dwarf planet.

There are **4** main rules for a dwarf planet.

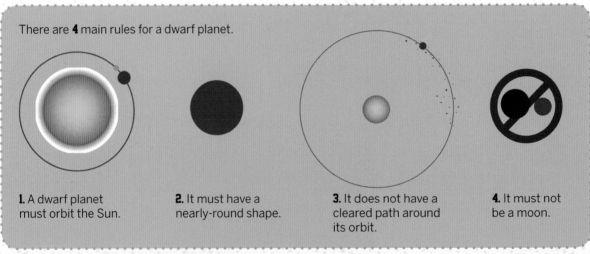

1. A dwarf planet must orbit the Sun.

2. It must have a nearly-round shape.

3. It does not have a cleared path around its orbit.

4. It must not be a moon.

Dwarf planets are all smaller than Mercury, which has a width of **3,032 mi (4,879 km)**.

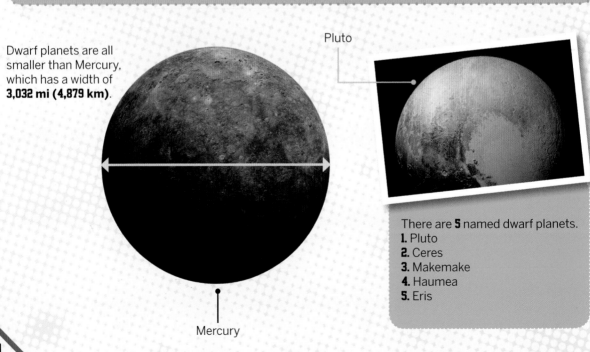

Pluto

Mercury

There are **5** named dwarf planets.
1. Pluto
2. Ceres
3. Makemake
4. Haumea
5. Eris

Ceres has a diameter of **591.5 mi (952 km)**, which means Earth is **13** times wider. This dwarf planet is the largest object in the Asteroid Belt (see page **56**).

Ceres

Ceres is the first dwarf planet that a spacecraft has orbited. NASA's Dawn probe reached it in **2015** and has traveled about **17,398 mi (28,000 km)** above its surface.

Dawn probe

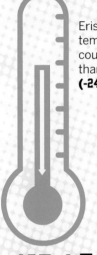

Eris' surface temperature could be lower than **-405.4°F (-243°C)**.

-405.4°F
(-243°C)

25%

Scientists think Ceres could have lots of water ice below its surface and that this maybe makes up **25 PERCENT** of the dwarf planet. This means it would have more water than all of the fresh water on Earth.

NUMBER CRUNCH
There could be over **100** dwarf planets waiting to be discovered by astronomers.

Haumea is slightly elongated (like a rugby ball) because it spins very fast. It completes **1** full spin in about **4 HOURS**, which makes it the fastest-spinning large object in the solar system.

Eris has a width of **1,445.3 mi (2,326 km)**. It has a moon called Dysnomia, which is less than **1/3** its size and moves around Eris once every **16 DAYS**.

Makemake was officially recognized as a dwarf planet in **2008**. It has a single moon, about **99.4 mi (160 km)** across.

In contrast to Haumea, dwarf planet **2007 OR10** is one of the slowest-spinning objects to orbit the Sun. It takes nearly **45 HOURS** to complete **1** spin.

2007 OR10 is the largest object in our solar system that has not yet received an official name. It has a diameter of **954 mi (1,535 km)**.

OUR MAGNIFICENT MOON

The easiest thing to spot in the night sky and, apart from the Earth, the most explored and studied object in our solar system is our Moon!

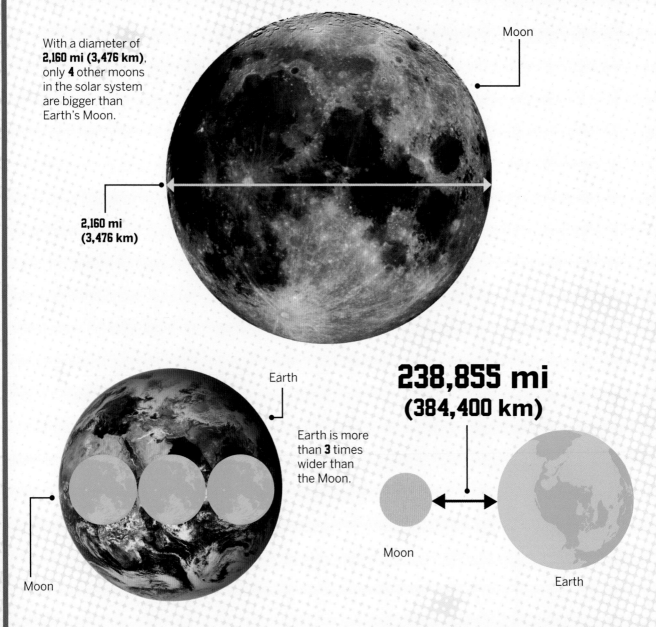

With a diameter of **2,160 mi (3,476 km)**, only **4** other moons in the solar system are bigger than Earth's Moon.

Moon

2,160 mi (3,476 km)

Earth

Earth is more than **3** times wider than the Moon.

Moon

238,855 mi (384,400 km)

Moon

Earth

The average distance between Earth and the Moon is **238,855 mi (384,400 km)**. It is the closest natural object to our planet. The distance between them varies between **221,457 mi (356,400 km)** and **252,712 mi (406,700 km)**.

 **x 30**

About **30** Earths could fit in the space between Earth and the Moon.

The Moon was probably formed around **4.5 BILLION YEARS** ago after a huge asteroid smashed into Earth and the flying debris from the collision came together to form the Moon.

1.5 in (3.78 cm)

The Moon is very slowly spinning away from Earth at a rate of about **1.5 in (3.78 cm)** each year.

In December **1968**, America's Apollo **8** mission was the first time humans had entered the Moon's orbit and returned to Earth safely. They circled the Moon **10** times on Christmas Eve and took a famous photograph of Earth, known as "Earthrise."

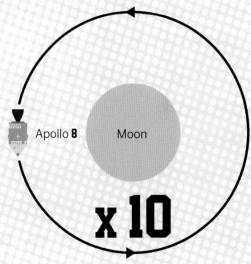

Apollo **8**   Moon

x 10

American astronauts brought **842 lbs (382 kg)** of Moon rocks, sand, and pebbles back to Earth to study in **2,200** separate samples. That's about the weight of **5** adults.

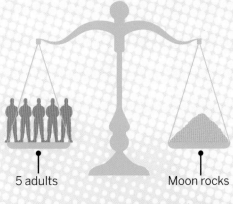

5 adults

Moon rocks

GRAVITY ÷ 6

Gravity on the Moon is only about **¹/₆** of what it is on Earth. That's why astronauts bounced on the surface during Moon walks in the 1960s and 1970s.

253.4°F (123°C)   **-369.4°F (-223°C)**

The surface temperature of the Moon can range from a freezing **-369.4°F (-223°C)** in darkness to a sizzling **253.4°F (123°C)** when the Moon is in daylight.

UNDER THE MOONLIGHT

Although the Moon seems very different from our blue planet, the links between them are fascinating.

The Apollo missions, using a Saturn rocket, took about **3 DAYS** to reach the Moon. If a normal **747** plane could fly to the Moon, it would take approximately **17 DAYS**!

747

17 DAYS

Earth

Moon

There are thousands of craters on the Moon's surface, caused by asteroids and comets crashing into it hundreds of millions of years ago. The Earth only has about **180** known craters, but the movement of the Earth's crust can remove evidence of these craters.

Crater

There are **2** main reasons why the Moon has so many craters...

1. Thin atmosphere doesn't stop objects from crashing into the surface.

2. No weather (wind or rain) erodes and changes the craters.

The famous Tycho crater is **53 mi (85 km)** in diameter and, when seen from Earth, seems to have bright rays coming from its center. These lighter areas were caused by rocks being thrown from the impact site about **108 MILLION YEARS** ago.

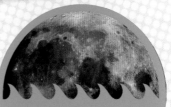

Tycho crater

17%

When viewed from Earth, the darker, smoother surfaces of the Moon are called maria. These are ancient volcanic plains and cover about **17 PERCENT** of the Moon's surface.

The Moon's gravitational pull causes tides in waters on Earth. Water "moves up" and creates a high tide at the points when that part of Earth is closest and farthest away from the Moon.

There are **2** high tides and **2** low tides all around the world on most days.

35,387 ft (10,786 m)

29,029 ft (8,848 m)

There could be as much as **13 trillion lbs (6 trillion kg)** of water ice below the Moon's surface. If the water could be mined and collected, then humans could maybe one day live on the Moon for long periods of time.

Mount Everest

Selenean summit

The highest point on the Moon is **35,387 ft (10,786 m)** above the surface, which is **6,358 ft (1,938 m)** more than Mount Everest on Earth. It's called the Selenean summit and has gentle slopes compared to Everest's steep sides.

1. A total lunar eclipse happens when the Moon and Sun are on opposite sides of Earth so that the Moon is in shadow. It then appears red.

Eclipses can last for a few hours and **2** or **3** partial eclipses happen each year. NASA has worked out that there will be **85** total lunar eclipses between the years **2001** and **2100**.

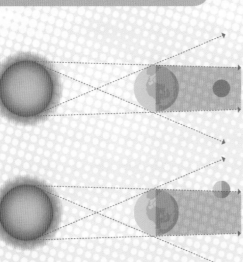

There are **2** main types of lunar (Moon) eclipse – a total eclipse and a partial eclipse.

2. A partial lunar eclipse happens when only part of the Moon is in Earth's shadow.

MORE MARVELOUS MOONS

Which moon has been described as a giant cheese pizza?
Get stuck into these tasty stats and you'll soon find out!

Jupiter has **69** known moons and **1** is the biggest in the solar system!

Ganymede

Ganymede has a diameter of **3,270 mi (5,262 km)** and is bigger than Mercury and Pluto. It is **2.4** times wider than Earth.

Ganymede and Jupiter's **3** other largest moons, called Io, Europa, and Callisto, were discovered by Galileo Galilei in **1610**. They were the first moons seen orbiting a planet other than ours.

Galileo Galilei

NUMBER CRUNCH
There are **175** moons that orbit planets in the solar system.

Callisto's light and dark areas and thousands of craters make it look like a glittering disco ball. Experts think the sparkling areas are mainly ice and its landscape is the oldest in the solar system at about **4 BILLION YEARS** old.

Io's volcanic plumes can rise **186 mi (300 km)** from the surface. NASA describes Io as looking like a giant pizza covered with melted cheese!

Io

x **400**

Io probably has over **400** volcanoes on its surface—more than any other object that we know of.

The first (and only) human-made object to land on a moon other than Earth's Moon was a **8.9 ft (2.7 m)**-wide circular spacecraft called the Huygens probe. It landed on Saturn's moon Titan in **2005**.

Huygens probe

The Huygens probe took over **7 YEARS** to reach Titan. It was attached to the Cassini spacecraft, which launched in **1997**.

Cassini

Huygens probe

Neptune's largest moon, Triton, is **1,682 mi (2,707 km)** wide. Scientists discovered its surface can be **-391°F (-235°C)**—**200** degrees colder than most household freezers.

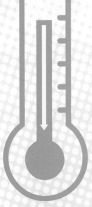

x **10**

-391°F (-235°C)

Pluto's largest moon, Charon, is **20** times closer to the planet than our Moon is to Earth. The **2** objects are just **12,204 mi (19,640 km)** apart.

Earth

Moon

x **20**

Pluto

Charon

AMAZING ASTEROID BELT

Home to hundreds of millions of floating space rocks, the Asteroid Belt is a vast area between the inner and outer planets. Let's take a trip through this spectacular zone!

Asteroids are rocks and rubble left over from when the solar system formed about **4.5 BILLION YEARS** ago.

Asteroids can be just **33 ft (10 m)** wide, but the largest is called Vesta and is **329 mi (530 km)** wide.

There are billions of asteroids orbiting the Sun in a huge zone called the Asteroid Belt. This lies between Mars and Jupiter and is about **93 million mi (150 million km)** wide.

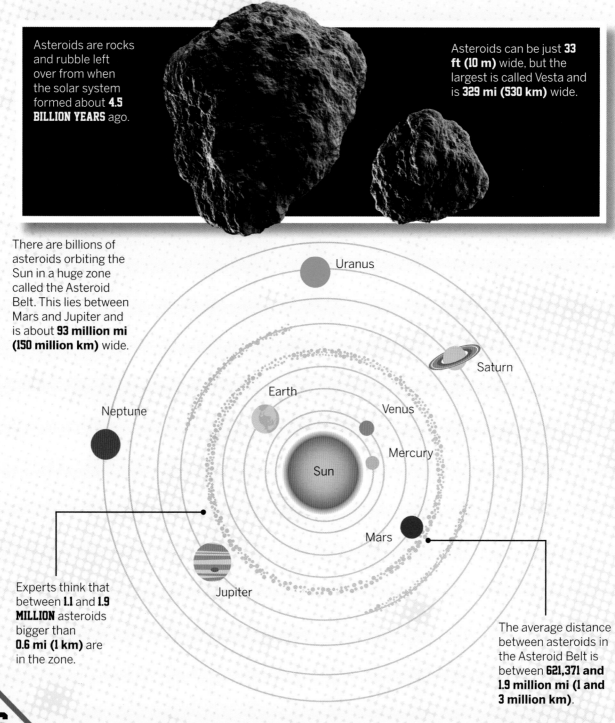

Experts think that between **1.1** and **1.9 MILLION** asteroids bigger than **0.6 mi (1 km)** are in the zone.

The average distance between asteroids in the Asteroid Belt is between **621,371 and 1.9 million mi (1 and 3 million km)**.

**4.7 million mi
(7.5 million km)**

NASA calls an asteroid that comes within **4.7 million mi (7.5 million km)** of Earth, and is bigger than **492 ft (150 m)**, a potential danger.

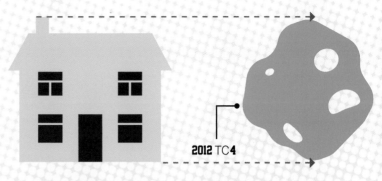

2012 TC4

In October **2017** an asteroid called **2012 TC4** was **36,039.5 mi (58,000 km)** from Earth. It was the size of a house.

2.4 million mi
(3.8 million km)

If an asteroid comes within about **2.4 million mi (3.8 million km)** of Earth's orbit, it's called a near-Earth asteroid (NEA).

Over **15,000** NEAs have been identified, with about **30** being spotted each week.

Ceres

The largest object in the Asteroid Belt is actually a dwarf planet called Ceres, at **590-mi (950-km)**-wide. It was observed and called an asteroid in **1801** before officially becoming a dwarf planet in **2006**.

Tunguska

An asteroid that could have been at least **197-ft (60-m)**-wide smashed into Earth in **1908**. It struck in Tunguska, Russia. Approximately **80 MILLION** trees were burnt or flattened by the impact across **772 square mi (2,000 square km)**.

When a giant asteroid or comet struck Earth **65 MILLION YEARS** ago, the collision led to the mass extinction of most dinosaurs. A crater **112 mi (180 km)** wide can be found where it struck, off the coast of Mexico.

CATCH UP WITH COMETS

Spotting a comet in the night sky, with a glowing tail and bright head, is a top treat. Here you'll discover some cool comet facts, plus more on meteors and meteoroids.

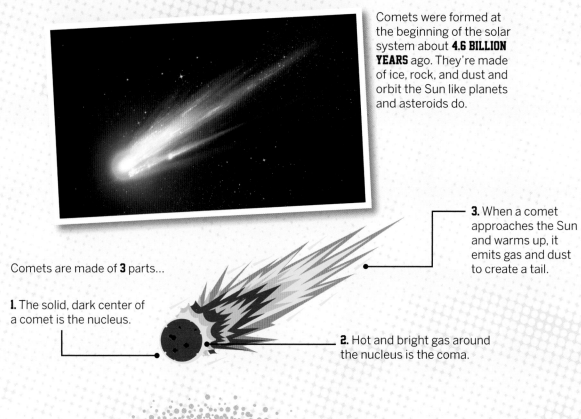

Comets were formed at the beginning of the solar system about **4.6 BILLION YEARS** ago. They're made of ice, rock, and dust and orbit the Sun like planets and asteroids do.

Comets are made of **3** parts...

1. The solid, dark center of a comet is the nucleus.

2. Hot and bright gas around the nucleus is the coma.

3. When a comet approaches the Sun and warms up, it emits gas and dust to create a tail.

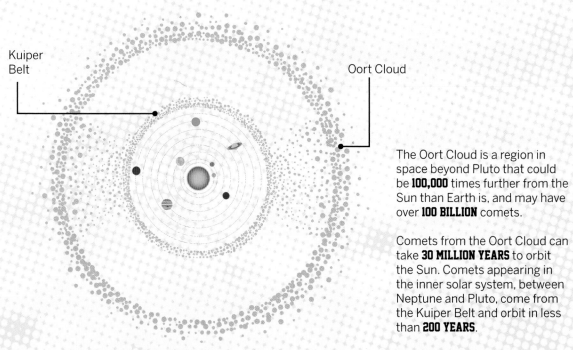

Kuiper Belt

Oort Cloud

The Oort Cloud is a region in space beyond Pluto that could be **100,000** times further from the Sun than Earth is, and may have over **100 BILLION** comets.

Comets from the Oort Cloud can take **30 MILLION YEARS** to orbit the Sun. Comets appearing in the inner solar system, between Neptune and Pluto, come from the Kuiper Belt and orbit in less than **200 YEARS**.

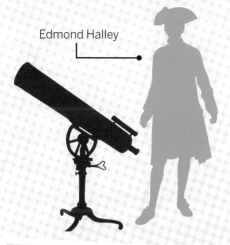

Edmond Halley

In **1705**, Edmond Halley worked out that comets seen from Earth in **1456**, **1531**, **1607**, and **1682** were actually the same comet returning. When the comet was seen again in **1758**, as he predicted, it became known as Halley's comet.

Halley's comet was last seen in **1986** and will be visible again in **2061**. The comet returns every **75** or **76 YEARS**.

NUMBER CRUNCH
It will take the Voyager spacecraft about another **300** years to reach the Oort Cloud and maybe **30,000** years to fly beyond it!

Bayeux Tapestry

An image of Halley's comet appears on the historic **11TH-CENTURY** Bayeux Tapestry, which shows the Battle of Hastings in **1066**.

The comet is about **9-mi (15-km)**-long and **5-mi (8-km)**-wide.

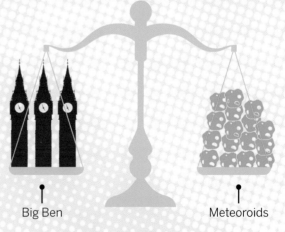

Philea probe

In **2014**, after **10 YEARS** of traveling, a small probe called Philea became the first to land on a comet and return information to Earth. The comet it reached was called **67**P/Churyumov-Gerasimenko.

Meteors, also called shooting stars, happen when small meteoroid rocks travel through Earth's atmosphere and burn up. The glow lasts for around **1 SECOND** at a height of about **47 to 62 mi (75 to 100 km)** from Earth's surface.

Big Ben

Meteoroids

A shooting star as seen from the International Space Station.

As much as **97,003 lbs (44,000 kg)** of meteoroids fall toward Earth every day. That's more than **3** times the weight of Big Ben in London.

SUPER STARS

Stars really are the leading lights of the universe! Earth's nearest star, the Sun, gives us light and energy and there are billions more out there. Get ready to crunch some extraordinary numbers!

There are **HUNDREDS** of **BILLIONS** of stars in our galaxy. Stars are constantly being created. How long they live depends on their mass and the nuclear fuel they contain. The bigger the star, the shorter its life.

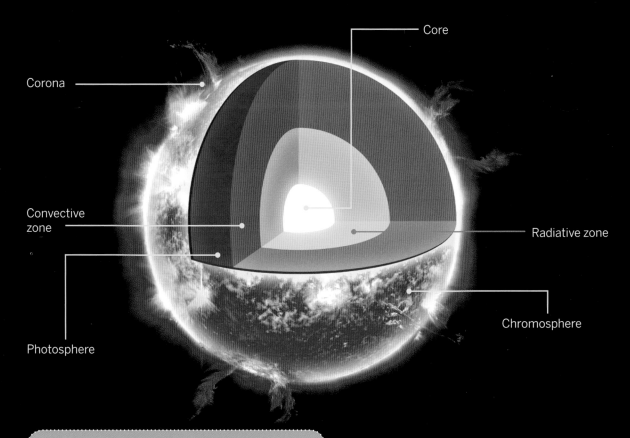

Core

Corona

Convective zone

Radiative zone

Chromosphere

Photosphere

4 MILLION YEARS
As a rough guide, a star with **15** times more mass than the Sun may live for just **4,000,000 YEARS**.

100 BILLION YEARS
A star with half the Sun's mass may burn for **100 BILLION YEARS**.

Stars form when clouds of gas and dust up to **93 million mi (150 million km)** wide begin to shrink and break up. Reaching **18 million °F (10 million °C)**, nuclear reactions take place to create a star.

Open cluster Taurus

Most stars belong to a group, called a cluster, of stars that were born at the same time. There are **2** common types...

1. Open clusters are younger and have fewer stars, so they look scattered.

2. Globular clusters are older, with many more stars, so they have a more distinct shape.

Viewed from Earth, some stars appear to form patterns or pictures in the sky, called constellations. There are **88** well known ones, including Orion, Taurus, Ursa Major, and Canis Major.

Ursa Major

There are **8** main colors of stars, with different average surface temperatures...

1. Green-white **64,832°F (36,000°C)**
2. Blue **51,512°F (28,600°C)**
3. White **19,292°F (10,700°C)**
4. Yellow-white **13,532°F (7,500°C)**
5. Yellow **11,732°F (6,500°C)**
6. Orange **8,672°F (4,800°C)**
7. Orange-red **6,152°F (3,400°C)**
8. Red **4,532°F (2,500°C)**

After the Sun, the nearest star to Earth is called Proxima Centauri. It's about **25 trillion mi (40 trillion km)** away—roughly **270,000** times further than the distance between Earth and the Sun.

Proxima Centauri

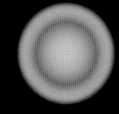

A spacecraft moving at a speedy **52,195 mph (84,000 km/h)** would still take **54,400 YEARS** to reach Proxima Centauri.

A star called R136a1 is thought to be about **9 MILLION** times more luminous than the Sun. Luminous means the amount of light it gives out.

GOING INTERGALACTIC

With billions of them in the universe, galaxies are home to trillions of stars. How much do you know about the Milky Way, Andromeda, and other glorious galaxies?

200 BILLION STARS

Stars are grouped together by gravity in a galaxy. There are over **200 BILLION** stars in our galaxy, the Milky Way, and there could be as many as **2 TRILLION** other galaxies!

The Milky Way is more than **100,000 LIGHT YEARS** in diameter. A light year is equal to about **5.9 trillion mi (9.5 trillion km)**. The Milky Way was formed about **13.6 BILLION YEARS** ago. At least **40** galaxies, including the Milky Way, are part of a cluster known as the Local Group.

Milky Way

Andromeda

Andromeda is the other large galaxy in the Local Group. It's predicted that in **4 BILLION YEARS** it will collide with the Milky Way.

Andromeda moves at over **248,548 mph (400,000 km/h)**—quick enough to travel from Earth to the Moon in under **1 HOUR**! If humans could travel at **10.7 mps (17.3 km/s)**, it would take **40 BILLION YEARS** to reach Andromeda—much longer than the universe has even existed.

It's **2.5 MILLION LIGHT YEARS** from the Milky Way, but Andromeda can be seen from Earth without a telescope, particularly during November.

Galaxies are one of these **4** shapes...

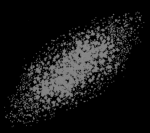

1. Elliptical galaxies—like a ball or egg

2. Spiral galaxies—like a disc, with a central bulge and arms spiraling out

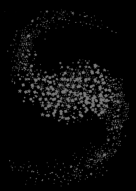

3. Barred-spiral galaxies—like spirals but with arms arcing out from a central bar shape

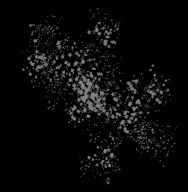

4. Irregular galaxies—with no pattern or regular shape

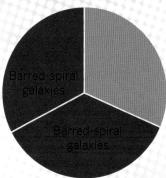

Barred-spiral galaxies

Barred-spiral galaxies

About **TWO THIRDS** of known galaxies are spiral or barred-spiral in shape.

220 MILLION YEARS

All objects in a galaxy revolve around its center. In the Milky Way galaxy, **1** revolution can take approximately **220 MILLION YEARS**.

Messier **51** is the technical name for a pretty galaxy also known as the Whirlpool because of its amazing spiraling arms of stars and gas. It was discovered in **1773** and is **30 MILLION LIGHT YEARS** from Earth.

At the center of all large galaxies are supermassive black holes. Black holes have so much gravity that they pull in everything nearby, including light. The Milky Way's black hole, Sagittarius A*, has the same mass as **4 MILLION** Suns.

AWESOME ASTRONOMERS

These amazing men and women are just a handful of the super-smart scientists to have discovered planets, stars, and many other wonders of the universe. We salute these awesome astronomers!

In **1515** a Polish astronomer called Nicolaus Copernicus correctly came up with the idea that planets orbited the Sun. At the time, most experts thought all objects orbited the Earth.

Copernicus didn't make his ideas public until **28 YEARS** later because he was worried about how people would react.

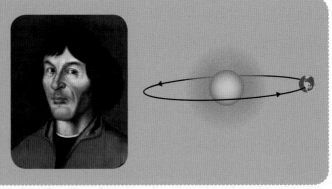

Thomas Harriot was the first astronomer to sketch and map the Moon by looking through a telescope. Harriot's drawings, in **1609** and **1610**, came **4 MONTHS** before Galileo's first Moon sketches using a telescope.

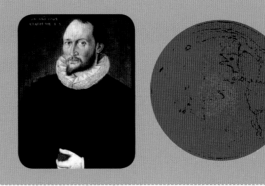

Galileo Galilei, born in **1564**, was an Italian who studied the stars and planets. He improved the telescope and discovered **4** of Jupiter's moons.

Galileo didn't get everything right. In **1610** he saw the rings around Saturn but thought they were part of a **3**-planet system.

A clever German astronomer, Johannes Kepler, came up with **3** vital laws about space in the early **1600**s...

1. Planets move (orbit) in oval paths, not circles.

2. Planets move at different rates.

3. A planet's orbit depends on its distance from the Sun.

 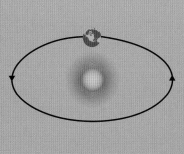

Englishman Isaac Newton, born in **1642**, published **3** important laws...

Law **I**—a moving object won't change speed or direction, and a still object won't move, unless a force acts on it.

Law **II**—the velocity (speed) of something changes when a force acts on it.

Law **III**—every action (force) has an equal and opposite reaction.

In the **18TH CENTURY**, the French astronomer Charles Messier wrote a detailed list of about **100** important objects and their positions in the sky. These were mainly galaxies, star clusters, and nebulae.

 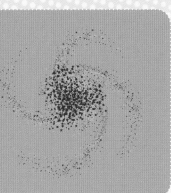

Caroline Herschel was an astronomer who, in the **18TH CENTURY**, with her brother William, built telescopes and discovered **8** comets.

On Caroline's **96TH** birthday she was given the King of Prussia's Gold Medal of Science.

William Herschel discovered Uranus in **1781**.

HIGH-FLYING HUBBLE

Named after American astronomer Edwin Hubble, the hi-tech Hubble Space Telescope is a mesmerizing machine orbiting high above Earth.

340 mi (547 km)

Orbiting Earth at **340 mi (547 km)** above the surface, the Hubble Space Telescope zooms around the planet in just **95 MINUTES** at a speed of **16,963 mph (27,300 km/h)**. That's like going from the east coast of America to the west coast in **10 MINUTES**.

Hubble was launched in **1990** by the space shuttle Discovery. By the end of **2017**, it had flown over **4 billion mi (6 billion km)** and made more than **1.3 MILLION** observations of the universe.

Hubble Space Telescope

It cost about **1.5 BILLION US DOLLARS**.

$1.5 BILLION

Telescopes on Earth suffer because the atmosphere blocks light. Unlike other ground-based telescopes, Hubble is above the atmosphere and can collect about **40,000** times more light than a human eye.

Hubble is **43.3-ft (13.2-m)**-long, **13.8 ft (4.2 m)** in diameter, and weighs **24,493 lbs (11,110 kg)**. The International Space Station is **8** times longer.

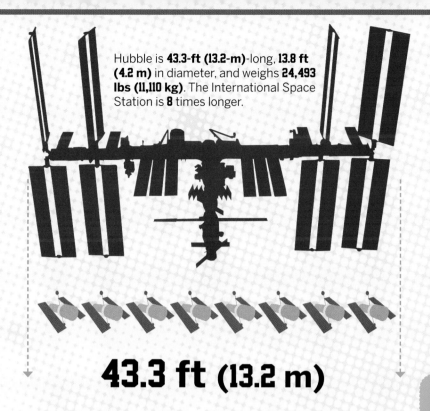

43.3 ft (13.2 m)

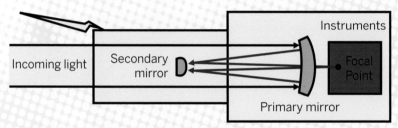

The primary mirror is **7.9 ft (2.4 m)** in diameter and the secondary mirror is **12 in (30 cm)**. Light bounces off the primary mirror to the secondary, then back through a hole in the primary.

Incoming light — Secondary mirror — Instruments — Focal Point — Primary mirror

LIGHT

Hubble's cameras can see **3** types of light – near-ultraviolet, visible, and near-infrared light.

Infrared light

Visible light

Ultraviolet light

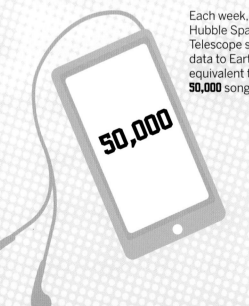

Each week, the Hubble Space Telescope sends data to Earth equivalent to **50,000** songs.

50,000

GN-z11

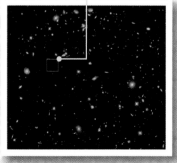

Hubble has detected the farthest galaxy ever found in the universe. Called GN-z11, it is seen as it was **13.4 BILLION YEARS** ago—just **400 MILLION YEARS** after the Big Bang that is thought to have brought the universe into being.

TERRIFIC TELESCOPES

Telescopes give us an exciting window into the solar system, whether from ground-based devices or hi-tech designs like the James Webb Space Telescope. Peer through these terrific telescope tales...

In **1608**, the first basic telescope is thought to have been created by a Dutchman called Hans Lippershey. Early telescopes were often called spyglasses and used lenses instead of mirrors.

Basic telescope

It would be another **60 YEARS** until Englishman Sir Isaac Newton built his powerful reflecting telescope that did use mirrors.

Reflecting telescope

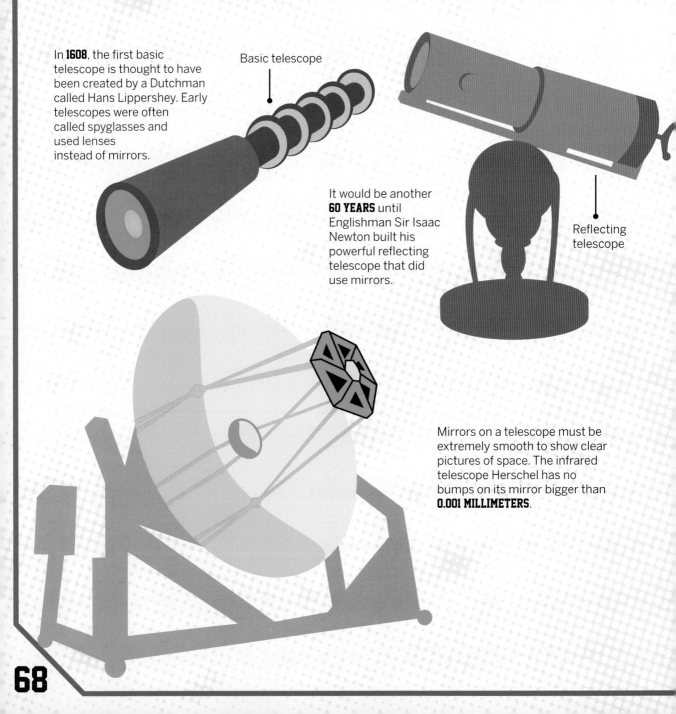

Mirrors on a telescope must be extremely smooth to show clear pictures of space. The infrared telescope Herschel has no bumps on its mirror bigger than **0.001 MILLIMETERS**.

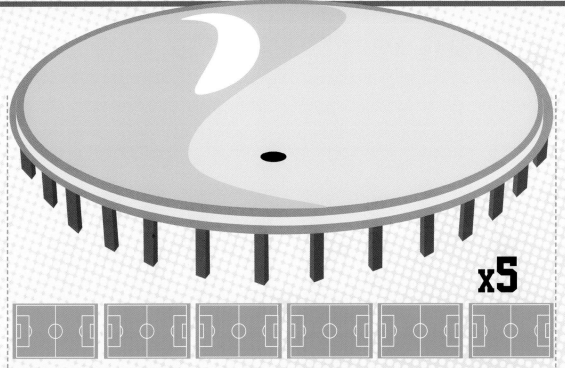

x5

The world's biggest ground-based, single-dish radio telescope is the Five Hundred Meter Aperture Spherical Telescope (FAST). It has a diameter of **1,640 ft (500 m)**, nearly **5** times longer than the soccer field at Wembley Stadium, London. The telescope is in China and the dish is made of **4,450** panels.

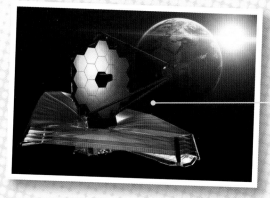

James Webb Space Telescope

Webb can observe **100** space objects at the same time.

The Extremely Large Telescope (ELT) will begin imaging the universe from Earth in **2024**. From its base in Chile **9,993 mi (3,046 m)** above sea level, ELT's record-breaking **128-ft (39-m)** primary mirror will be made of nearly **800** hexagonal pieces.

Due to be launched in **2019**, the impressive James Webb Space Telescope will have a **21-ft (6.5-m)** primary mirror—nearly **3** times bigger than Hubble's.

x 3

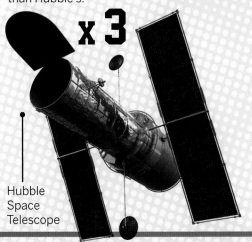

Hubble Space Telescope

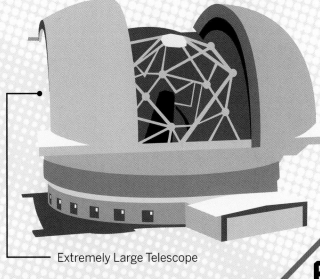

Extremely Large Telescope

FLYING INTO SPACE

Exploring space is only possible because of the spectacular and sophisticated machines that can reach Earth's orbit and beyond. Here's a countdown to some of the coolest spacecraft ever!

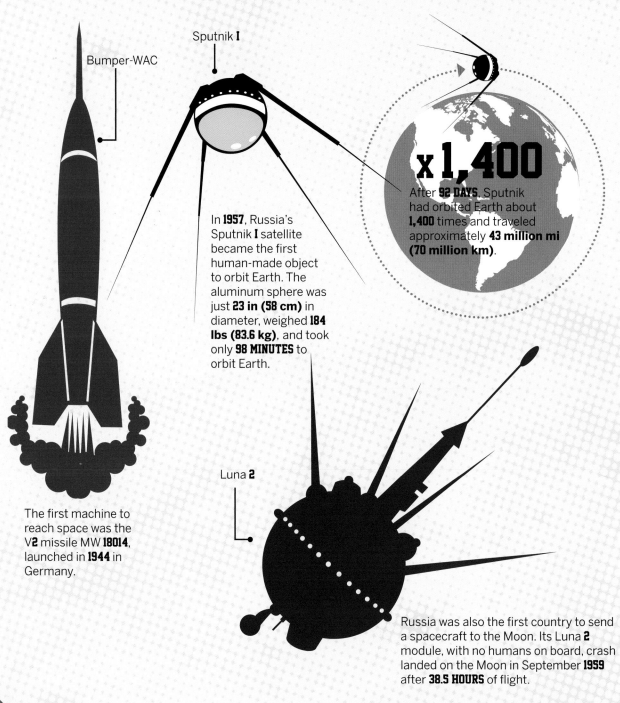

Bumper-WAC

Sputnik **I**

In **1957**, Russia's Sputnik **I** satellite became the first human-made object to orbit Earth. The aluminum sphere was just **23 in (58 cm)** in diameter, weighed **184 lbs (83.6 kg)**, and took only **98 MINUTES** to orbit Earth.

x1,400

After **92 DAYS**, Sputnik had orbited Earth about **1,400** times and traveled approximately **43 million mi (70 million km)**.

The first machine to reach space was the V**2** missile MW **18014**, launched in **1944** in Germany.

Luna **2**

Russia was also the first country to send a spacecraft to the Moon. Its Luna **2** module, with no humans on board, crash landed on the Moon in September **1959** after **38.5 HOURS** of flight.

In **1977** NASA launched the Voyager **1** and Voyager **2** spacecraft ... and they are still traveling now! By the end of **2017**, Voyager **1** was more than **13 billion mi (21 billion km)** from Earth and Voyager **2** was over **10.6 billion mi (17 billion km)** away.

The Voyager **2** spacecraft is the only machine to fly by Jupiter, Saturn, Uranus, and Neptune. It is expected to be able to send information back to Earth until the year **2025**.

Voyager 1

Eagle

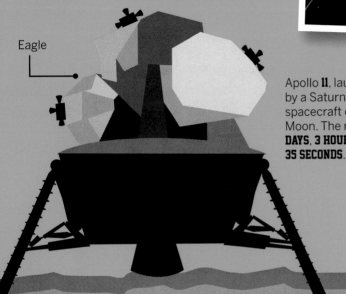

Apollo **11**, launched in July **1969** by a Saturn **V** rocket, landed a spacecraft called Eagle on the Moon. The mission lasted for **8 DAYS, 3 HOURS, 18 MINUTES**, and **35 SECONDS**.

Cassini

The fastest geocentric speed (speed relative to Earth) of an active spacecraft was set by Juno in **2016**. It hit an amazing **164,663 mph (265,000 km/h)**.

LANDINGS

Spacecraft have landed or crashed onto **5** planets – Jupiter, Mercury, Venus, Mars, and Saturn.

Mercury

Venus

Jupiter

Mars

Saturn

In September **2017**, after **20 YEARS** of exploring the solar system, the Cassini spacecraft was deliberately crashed into Saturn. Cassini...

• Orbited Saturn **294** times since **2004**.

• Took **453,048** images.

• Flew **4.9 billion mi (7.9 billion km)**.

• Cost **3.9 BILLION US DOLLARS**.

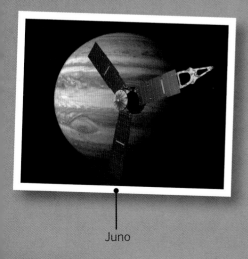

Juno

SPECTACULAR SPACECRAFT

Satellites, Space Shuttles, Soyuz, and even super-expensive Moon vehicles have helped us discover space stats!

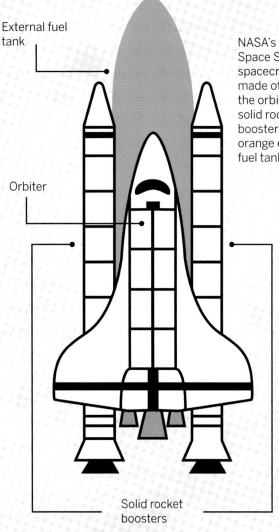

External fuel tank

Orbiter

Solid rocket boosters

NASA's famous Space Shuttle spacecraft was made of **3** parts—the orbiter, twin solid rocket boosters, and an orange external fuel tank.

$113.7 BILLION

The Space Shuttle's **30-YEAR** mission has cost **113.7 BILLION US DOLLARS**.

The Space Shuttle orbited Earth between **115 and 398 mi (185 and 640 km)** above the surface and reached speeds of about **17,398 mph (28,000 km/h)**.

The **84-ft-long (56-m-long)** spacecraft spent a total of **1,334 DAYS** in space and flew over **542 million mi (873 million km)**. It carried between **2** and **8** astronauts at a time.

On the last **3** of NASA's missions to the Moon, astronauts drove a Lunar Roving Vehicle on the surface. Nicknamed "the Moon buggy", **3** were driven on the Moon over a distance of **56 mi (90 km)**.

McLaren P1 supercar

$38 MILLION

The Moon buggy is thought to be the most expensive vehicle ever built, costing **38 MILLION US DOLLARS** – about **33** times more expensive than a modern McLaren P1 supercar!

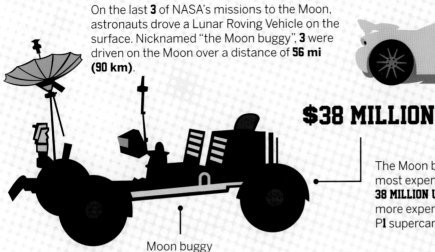

Moon buggy

The Russian Soyuz spacecraft has made over **1,680** launches since **1967**. It takes up to **3** astronauts to the International Space Station on each flight.

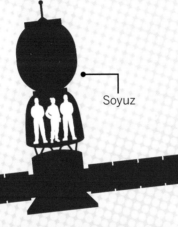

Soyuz

35 ft (10.6 m)

The Soyuz is **23-ft (7-m)**-long and **9 ft (2.7 m)** in diameter. When its solar panels are open in space, these are **35-ft (10.6-m)**-wide.

Soyuz reaches Earth's orbit **8 MINUTES** and **45 SECONDS** after launch.

8 MINUTES 45 SECONDS

There are thought to be over **4,635** satellites orbiting Earth. Satellites send messages and data around the world and monitor all sorts of things, such as weather, oceans, planes, and traffic.

Satellites are usually taken into space by rockets and can orbit in one of **3** zones...

1. Low-Earth orbit—**112 to 1,243 mi (180 to 2,000 km)** above Earth
2. Mid-Earth orbit—**1,243 to 22,233 mi (2,000 to 35,780 km)**
3. High-Earth orbit—over **22,233 mi (35,780 km)**

The American Global Positioning System (GPS) uses **30** satellites. Many cars use GPS to send information to their satellite navigation (sat nav) devices.

THE INCREDIBLE ISS

The International Space Station (ISS) is probably the most amazing spacecraft ever constructed. It's mega fast, mega clever, and mega expensive—check out all this incredible ISS info!

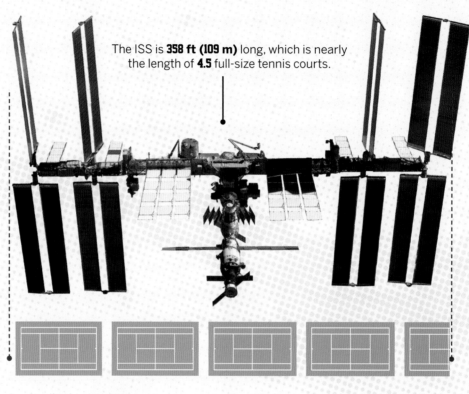

The ISS is **358 ft (109 m)** long, which is nearly the length of **4.5** full-size tennis courts.

ISS

Boeing **777**

The giant solar panels contain **262,400** solar cells covering an area of **26,910 square ft (2,500 square m)**. These can generate **120 KILOWATTS** of electricity, which is enough energy to power **40** homes.

It has **8 PAIRS** of huge solar panels that have a length of **239.5 ft (73 m)**. That's longer than the wingspan of a Boeing **777** plane, which is **213 ft (65 m)**. Solar panels use sunlight to make power.

x 40

60%

When the ISS is in sunlight, **60 PERCENT** of the power from the solar panels is used to recharge the batteries. When the sunlight disappears, these batteries power the spacecraft.

Battery

Costing about **$100 BILLION**, the ISS is the most expensive single item ever constructed.

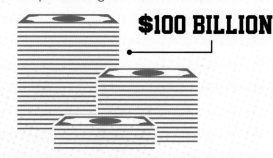

$100 BILLION

13 YEARS

The International Space Station took **13 YEARS** to build in space, between **1998** and **2011**.

The first piece of the ISS, the Zarya Control Module, was taken into space on **NOVEMBER 20, 1998** onboard a Russian Proton rocket.

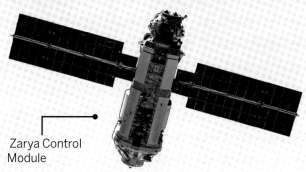

Zarya Control Module

15 nations helped to build this ISS.

 Belgium   Canada   Denmark   France

 Germany   Italy   Japan   Netherlands

 Norway   Russia   Spain   Sweden

 Switzerland   United Kingdom   United States of America

x 280

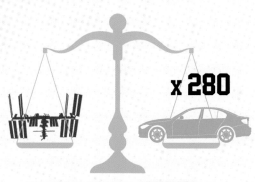

The ISS weighs about **925,942 lbs (420,000 kg)**—the equivalent of about **280** cars!

NUMBER CRUNCH
52 hi-tech on-board computers are needed to control the International Space Station.

The **55.8-ft (17-m)**-long robotic arm on the outside of the ISS is called **CANADARM 2**. It was built by the Canadian Space Agency and can lift about **253,531 lbs (115,000 kg)**

CANADARM 2

LIVING THE HIGH LIFE

Life on the International Space Station is pretty spectacular for the astronauts who work there. These lucky men and women spend several months at a time zooming around in space, high above Earth.

Astronauts on the ISS travel around the Earth at a height of about **248.5 mi (400 km)**.

The ISS moves at a speed of **17,150 mph (27,600 km/h)**. This means that each day it travels about the same distance as from Earth to the Moon... and back again!

Earth

Moon

17,150 mph
(27,600 km/h)

90 MINS

The ISS orbits (travels around) the Earth about once every **90 MINUTES**. On average the astronauts see **16** sunrises and sunsets every **24 HOURS.**

16

Russia's Soyuz capsule is now the only rocket that takes astronauts to and from the ISS. It can carry a maximum of **3** people and usually takes about **6 HOURS** to reach the ISS from Earth.

Soyuz

Soyuz is made of **3** parts – the Orbital Module, Descent Module and the Instrumentation Module. The Descent Module is the part astronauts are in during launch and landing.

When astronauts return to Earth, only the Descent Module lands. The other **2** parts burn up in the atmosphere. The return journey lasts about **3.5 HOURS**.

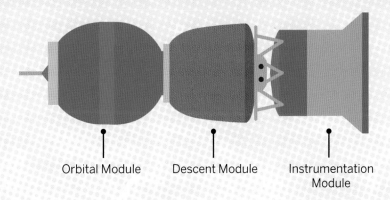

Orbital Module   Descent Module   Instrumentation Module

By **2017**, over **220** astronauts from **18** different countries had visited the ISS. The first **3** people arrived on **NOVEMBER 2, 2000**.

x 220

Astronaut

Spacewalks are when astronauts go outside the ISS in their special spacesuits. The longest ISS spacewalk was in **2001** and lasted **8 HOURS** and **56 MINUTES**. The shortest happened in **2009** and was just **12 MINUTES**.

8 HRS
56 MINS

The ISS has **3** international research laboratories and as many as **150** experiments can happen at once. Experiments have included trying to grow vegetables in space, how flames behave in space, and testing different types of sports shoes during exercise!

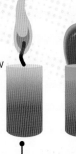

Earth   Space

There are only **2** toilets on the space station. They use a vacuum system to suck waste away and they cost about **$19 MILLION**—the most expensive toilets in the universe!

176°F (80°C)

2 HRS

Astronauts prepare their own meals and can heat food on the ISS, but the ovens only reach about **176°F (80°C)**.

Astronauts will spend an average of **35 HOURS** a week carrying out experiments and maintaining the ISS. They work **5 DAYS** a week and have weekends to relax.

The ISS crew wakes up around **6AM** and is busy until approximately **9.30PM**. The astronauts must work out for over **2 HOURS** each day to keep fit and healthy.

UP, UP, AND AWAY...

Astronauts have a job that is both amazing and frightening. Their mission is to launch into space and explore the unknown. Check out these epic astronaut numbers.

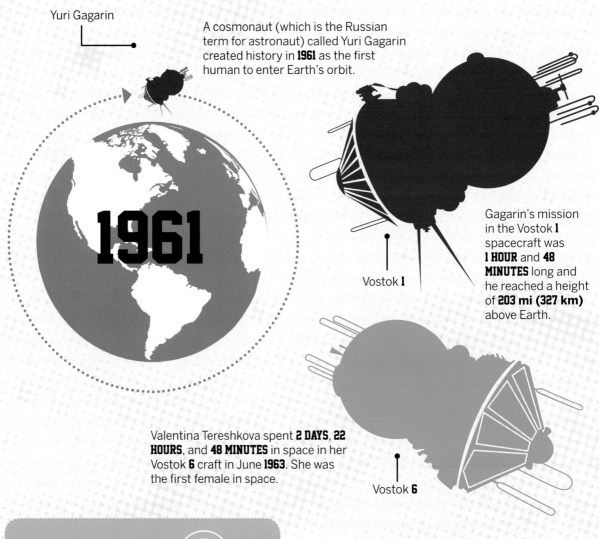

Yuri Gagarin

A cosmonaut (which is the Russian term for astronaut) called Yuri Gagarin created history in **1961** as the first human to enter Earth's orbit.

1961

Vostok **1**

Gagarin's mission in the Vostok **1** spacecraft was **1 HOUR** and **48 MINUTES** long and he reached a height of **203 mi (327 km)** above Earth.

Valentina Tereshkova spent **2 DAYS, 22 HOURS**, and **48 MINUTES** in space in her Vostok **6** craft in June **1963**. She was the first female in space.

Vostok **6**

Tereshkova married Andrian Nikolayev, another cosmonaut, and their daughter Elena was born in **1964**. Elena was the first child born to parents who had both been to space.

Only **12** male astronauts have ever walked on the Moon and they were all American.

1ST

Neil Armstrong was the first human to set foot on the Moon in July **1969** and Eugene Cernan was the last in December **1972**.

665 DAYS

In **2017**, Peggy Whitson set a record as the NASA astronaut with the longest time in space. In total she spent **665 DAYS** in Earth's orbit during **3** different missions.

12 MINS

Russia's Alexey Leonov spent **12 MINUTES** on the first ever spacewalk in March **1965**.

60 HRS 21 MINS

Peggy Whitson made **10** spacewalks that lasted **60 HOURS** and **21 MINUTES**.

77 YEARS

NASA astronaut John Glenn was **77** when, in October **1998**, he became the oldest person ever to fly in space.

Sadly **3** astronauts have died in space. In **1971** Georgi Dobrovolski, Vladislav Volkov, and Viktor Patsayev were in a Soyuz **11** capsule that depressurized before re-entry to Earth's atmosphere after **23 DAYS** in space.

879 DAYS

The most days spent in space by one person is **879**. Russia's Gennady Padalka set the record after completing his **FIFTH** space mission in **2015**.

SUITS YOU!

An astronaut's spacesuit is an amazing piece of technology. Without it, no human could have walked in space or on the Moon. Here are stacks of spacesuit stats, plus more amazing astronaut numbers.

-238°F (-150°C)   **248°F (120°C)**

A spacesuit protects an astronaut from temperatures ranging from **-238°F to 248°F (-150°C to 120°C)** while he or she is on a spacewalk.

14 LAYERS

The spacesuit arms have **14** layers, including a bulletproof layer designed as protection from flying space dust.

300 ft (91.5 m)

Under the spacesuit astronauts wear a full-length skin suit that has **300 ft (91.5 m)** of tubing. Water's pumped around the tubing to keep the astronaut cool in space.

280 lbs (127 kg)

A spacesuit can weigh **280 lbs (127 kg)** on Earth but weigh virtually zero in the microgravity of space.

On a typical spacewalk, an astronaut will handle between **70** and **110** different tools and pieces of equipment.

45 MINUTES

It takes **45 MINUTES** to put on a spacesuit.

1 HOUR+

Once inside a suit, an astronaut spends at least **1 HOUR** breathing pure oxygen before a spacewalk.

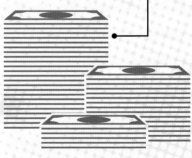

$22 MILLION

In the **1960**s it cost NASA about **22 MILLION US DOLLARS** to design and build its first spacesuit.

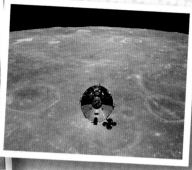

NUMBER CRUNCH
NASA Apollo **10** astronauts Thomas Stafford, John Young, and Eugene Cernan achieved the fastest human spaceflight record of **24,791 mph (39,897 km/h)** in **1969**.

Neutral Buoyancy Laboratory

60 million gallons
(23 million liters)

On Earth, NASA trains astronauts for spacewalks in a huge **60-million-gallon (23-million-liter)** water pool. The water helps create a feeling of weightlessness like in space.

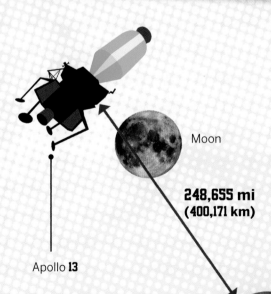

For every **1 HOUR** an astronaut will spend in space, he or she must train for **7 HOURS** in the pool.

1 HOUR = 7 HOURS

Moon

248,655 mi (400,171 km)

Apollo **13**

Apollo **13** astronauts Jim Lovell, Fred Haise, and Jack Swigert flew a record **248,655 mi (400,171 km)** away from Earth's surface when they passed the far side of the Moon in **1971**.

Earth

NASA: DID YOU KNOW?

NASA is the most famous space agency in the world, with a special place in the history of space flight, astronauts, and technology. Check out these nifty NASA numbers!

America's government space agency NASA (National Aeronautics and Space Administration) employs over **18,000** people and has an annual budget of **19.1 BILLION US DOLLARS**.

NUMBER CRUNCH
When NASA began in **1958**, it employed just **8,000** people, with an annual budget of only **100 MILLION US DOLLARS**.

$19.1 BILLION

x 10

Apollo **8**

NASA's Apollo **8** mission in December **1968** saw astronauts orbit the Moon for the first time. Jim Lovell, Frank Borman, and William Anders were in space for **6 DAYS**, **3 HOURS**, and **42 SECONDS**.

Moon

X 44 The number of active astronauts at NASA in **2017**.

280 The number of former astronauts who flew missions with NASA since 1958.

The **3** astronauts completed **10** Moon orbits and were the first humans to see the far side of the Moon.

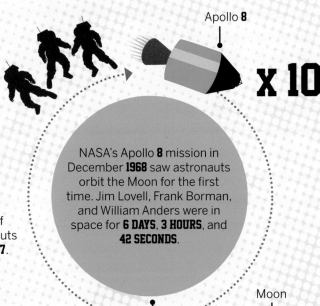

The most famous space mission in NASA's history is Apollo **11**, which took the first astronauts to the Moon on July **20**, **1969**.

Apollo **11**

530 MILLION

An estimated TV audience of **530 MILLION** people watched Neil Armstrong walk on the Moon and say, "one small step for a man, one giant leap for mankind."

NASA's most iconic spacecraft was the Space Shuttle. Between **1981** and **2011**, **5** Space Shuttles flew **133** missions carrying **355** different crew members.

Space Shuttle

In **1959**, NASA's Explorer **6** spacecraft was the first to photograph Earth from space.

The huge Vehicle Assembly Building (VAB) at NASA's Kennedy Space Center in Florida, USA, is **525-ft (160-m)**-tall, **518-ft (158-m)**-wide, and covers **27,508 sq yds (23,000 sq m)**.

The VAB will help create NASA's new Space Launch System, which could eventually take **4** astronauts on a deep-space mission to Mars in the **2030**s.

Mariner **2**

Venus

When it came within **21,127 mi (34,000 km)** of Venus in **1962**, NASA's Mariner **2** spacecraft was the first to "fly by" another planet and send data to Earth.

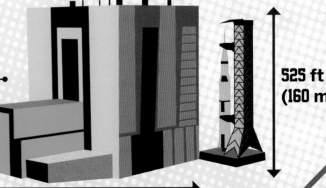

Vehicle Assembly Building

525 ft (160 m)

518 ft (158 m)

MORE SPECIAL AGENCIES

NASA is not the only space agency on the planet—many countries around the world have developed missions to explore the vast regions beyond planet Earth.

22

In total there are **22** nations that form the European Space Agency (ESA).

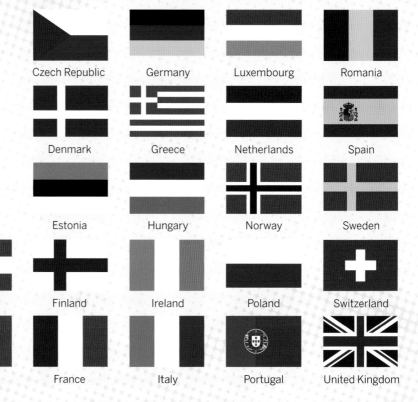

Czech Republic   Germany   Luxembourg   Romania

Denmark   Greece   Netherlands   Spain

Estonia   Hungary   Norway   Sweden

Austria   Finland   Ireland   Poland   Switzerland

Belgium   France   Italy   Portugal   United Kingdom

1975

The ESA was created in **1975** and its first astronaut went into space in **1983**.

More than **2,000** people are employed by the ESA. Its annual budget is around **5.75 BILLION EUROS (6.91 BILLION DOLLARS, at the current exchange rate of 1 EUR = 1.20 USD)**.

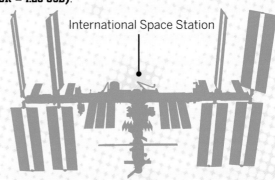

International Space Station

11 of the ESA countries, including the United Kingdom, France, Germany, Italy, and the Netherlands, worked with the United States, Russia, Canada, and Japan to build the International Space Station.

13.7 BILLION POUNDS
(18.5 BILLION USD, at the current exchange rate of 1 GBP = 1.35 USD)

NUMBER CRUNCH
China plans to have built its own space station by the early **2020**s, which will be about **1/6** the size of the ISS.

Apart from America, only **2** other countries have launched crewed (human occupied) missions into space. Russia first did so in **1961** and China in **2003**.

The amount of money that the United Kingdom's space industry generates for the British economy per year.

Tim Peake was the first Briton to fly to and live on the ISS in **2015**, as an ESA astronaut. He spent **186** days in space and orbited Earth **2,976** times.

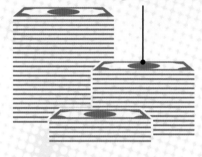

Japan's space agency, JAXA, monitors flying space debris at an altitude of **22,369 mi (36,000 km)**. In **1** year it can receive about **90,000** warnings that debris may collide with a satellite or spacecraft.

ROSCOSMOS is Russia's space agency. Its new Vostochny Cosmodrome has a **171-ft (52-m)**-high mobile service tower to launch rockets.

Vostochny Cosmodrome covers **212 square mi (550 square km)**, which is about a **3RD** of the size of London.

2 Canadian Space Agency astronauts have flown to the ISS and **8** astronauts went on **14** NASA Space Shuttle missions between **1984** and **2009**.

ANIMALS IN SPACE

At the beginning of the space age, animals were sometimes part of important missions. Thanks to these special creatures, humans began to understand what was needed to survive spaceflights and trips to the Moon.

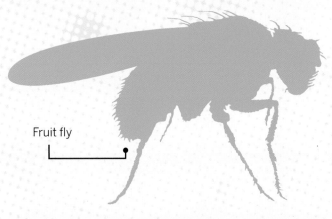

Fruit fly

America sent fruit flies **68 mi (109 km)** into space in February **1947**. The tiny creatures—about **2.5 MILLIMETERS** long—returned safely to Earth and were the first animals in space.

LIFESPAN

30 DAYS

Fruit flies have a natural lifespan of about **30 DAYS**.

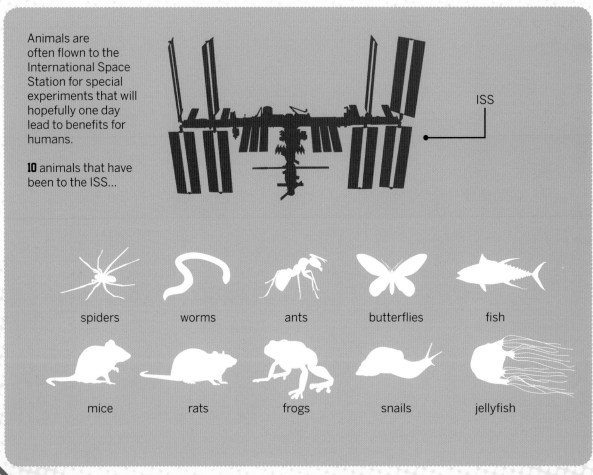

Animals are often flown to the International Space Station for special experiments that will hopefully one day lead to benefits for humans.

10 animals that have been to the ISS...

ISS

| spiders | worms | ants | butterflies | fish |

| mice | rats | frogs | snails | jellyfish |

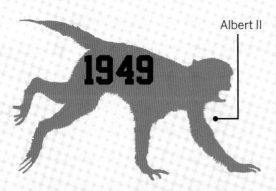

1949

Albert II

In **1949**, a monkey called Albert II flew into space inside a V-**2** Blossom rocket. It reached a height of **83 mi (134 km)**.

The first monkey to be recovered after a spaceflight was called Yorick. Along with **11** mice, the animals flew **45 mi (72 km)** high in **1951**.

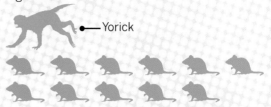

Yorick

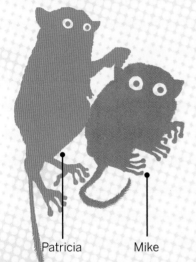

1,988 mph (3,200 km/h)—That's the speed **2** Philippine monkeys, Patricia and Mike, traveled at while they journeyed with a NASA rocket in **1952**.

Patricia   Mike

Between **1951** and **1952**, **9** special Russian dogs were part of space missions that failed to go into space, with **3** of them flying **TWICE**. The **FIRST** dog to actually enter space, in **1957**, was called Laika.

A total of **2,478** moon jellyfish went into space on the Columbia Space Shuttle. The population grew to about **60,000** while in Earth's orbit.

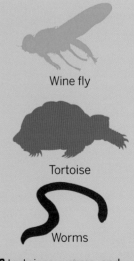

Wine fly

Tortoise

Worms

2 tortoises, worms, and wine flies were part of the Zond **5** Russian spaceflight in **1968**. They were the **FIRST** animals to go beyond Earth's orbit and they even circled the Moon.

A tiny micro-animal called a tardigrade, which is usually less than **1 MILLIMETER** long, existed for **10 DAYS** in open space in **2007**. Tardigrades can live in very cold and dry conditions.

IS THERE ANYBODY OUT THERE . . .?

Do aliens, UFOs, and simple life forms exist beyond Earth? So far scientists have found no proof, but that doesn't mean the exciting search will ever stop!

Below the ice on its surface, Jupiter's moon Europa could have **3** times more water than Earth has.

Europa

H₂O

Liquid water is essential for life as we know it. If it's found on other planets and objects, it means one day life may be found there, too.

Ceres

The American group Search for Extraterrestrial Intelligence (SETI) uses ground telescopes to search for signals that may have been sent by other life forms. Since it started in **1984**, SETI has discovered **0** signs of life beyond Earth.

In **2017**, evidence of organic molecules on the dwarf planet Ceres was discovered. These molecules are an important part of life on Earth and could suggest signs of past life on Ceres, too.

NASA says Venus, the second planet from the Sun, is often mistaken by star-gazers for a UFO because it can be so clear and bright in the night sky. A UFO is an Unidentified Flying Object.

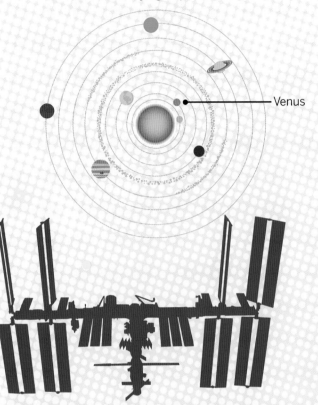

Venus

The most famous UFO case happened in **1947** when a pilot, Kenneth Arnold, reported seeing **9** flying disc-shaped objects in the sky. This led to the popular "flying saucer" image of UFOs.

DANGER UFOs

Also in **1947**, a UFO was reported to have crashed in New Mexico and stories of alien bodies being discovered at the site were made. It wasn't until **47 YEARS** later that NASA said the crash was actually a top-secret weather balloon.

YouTube videos thought to show UFOs flying past the ISS have had **HUNDREDS** of **THOUSANDS** of views. NASA says these objects are reflections from the ISS's windows or lights from Earth.

Earth

Mars

9 MONTHS

Mars is closer to Earth than most planets, but it would still take around **9 MONTHS** for humans to fly there. It's the planet that humans may one day be able to visit, but it doesn't have its own oxygen supply.

Scientists think Mars has lost about **87 PERCENT** of the water it had **BILLIONS OF YEARS** ago.

87%

13%

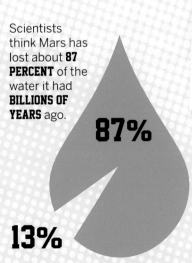

HD **40307**g is a distant planet that's estimated to be **56 million mi (90 million km)** from its star. This distance could mean it has a temperature that would support life.

UNBELIEVABLE ... BUT TRUE!

Get ready for some fun, ridiculous, cool, and totally stunning space stats and numbers!

The largest meteorite found on Earth weighs about **119,000 lbs (54,000 kg)** – the same as **10** large African elephants. The giant iron lump, called the Hoba meteorite, landed in Namibia, Africa, approximately **80,000 YEARS** ago.

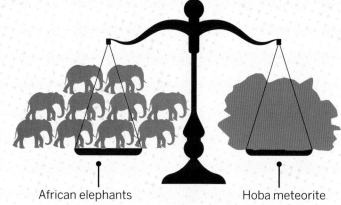

African elephants

Hoba meteorite

Humans are made from stardust! Our bodies are made from atoms and all atoms were made in stars **BILLIONS OF YEARS** ago. About **97 PERCENT** of a human's atoms are the same as those found in the Milky Way galaxy.

Even diagrams of atoms remind us of objects in space!

Fidget spinner

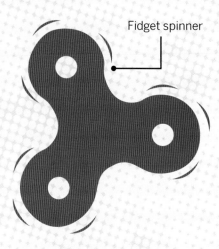

In **2017**, a video posted on Twitter showed **4** astronauts playing with a fidget spinner on the International Space Station. The cool clip shows the toy spinning by itself in zero gravity!

Dinosaurs died out after a giant asteroid or comet crashed into Earth **65 MILLION YEARS** ago, but amazingly a dinosaur has been in space! Fossils of a hadrosaur were taken on NASA's Space Shuttle in **1985**.

5 CM

ISS

Astronauts that spend many weeks living on the ISS can grow by up to **2 in (5 cm)** because there's no gravity pushing down on them. After about **10 DAYS** back on Earth they go back to their normal height.

Dennis Tito, an American billionaire, paid a reported **20 MILLION US DOLLARS** to become the first ever "space tourist" in **2001**. He flew to the ISS and spent **8 DAYS** in space.

Astronaut Alan Shepard hit a golf ball with a golf club on the Moon in **1971**. It has been calculated that the ball traveled about **2.5 mi (4 km)**—10 times farther than golf balls on Earth!

$20 MILLION

6 MONTHS

Because time for a fast-moving person passes at a different rate than for someone who is still, astronauts in space age slightly less than they would do on Earth. For every **6 MONTHS** in space, an astronaut ages **0.007 SECONDS** less!

The coldest known place in the universe is on the ISS. The Cold Atom Lab is a box that conducts experiments at **1 BILLIONTH OF A DEGREE** above **-459.67°F (-273.15°C)**, the temperature known as absolute zero and the lowest possible.

The Apollo **12** Saturn **V** rocket was struck by lightning just **36 SECONDS** after lift-off in **1969**. Amazingly, no damage was done and the mission continued and reached the Moon.

-459.67°F (-273.15°C)

INCREDIBLE ...
BUT ALSO TRUE!

Prepare for even more out-of-this-world space stats and numbers, including pizzas, Christmas trees, Nerf toys, and the quietest astronauts ever!

In **2001**, Pizza Hut paid **1 MILLION US DOLLARS** to send a salami pizza to the ISS. Russian cosmonaut Yuri Usachov enjoyed the tasty treat! The snack was sent aboard a rocket that had other supplies for the station.

Stashed away in a box on the ISS is a **21-in (60-cm)**-tall Christmas tree that astronauts take out and decorate every December.

24 in (60 cm)

One of the coolest jobs at NASA is being a Planetary Protection Officer, a position created in the **1960**s to deal with contamination in space... sadly, not to save the world from aliens!

Lonnie Johnson was a space engineer on the Galileo spacecraft mission to Jupiter in the **1980**s. He's more famous for creating the fun Super Soaker water pistol and Nerf dart toys!

Super Soaker

Buzz Aldrin was the second person to walk on the Moon in **1969**. Coincidentally, his mother's name was Marion Moon.

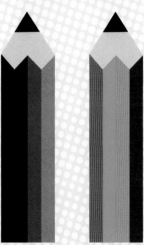

In the early **1960**s, astronauts used pencils to write in space because the ink in pens wouldn't flow with no gravity.

NUMBER CRUNCH
Over **100** countries have signed the Outer Space Treaty. This means that no nation can claim to own the planets, the Moon, or any part of space.

Even if they were able to stand face-to-face without spacesuits, **2** humans could not have a shouting match in space! There are no air molecules to vibrate and carry sound.

Gemini **6**

Gemini **7**

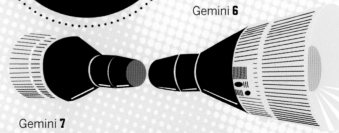

The Gemini **6** and Gemini **7** spacecraft flew within just **6 in (15 cm)** of each other in **1965**—the first space meeting. They proved that machines could connect with each other safely in space.

SPACE NUMBER CRUNCH QUICK QUIZ

You'll find the answers to all these number crunch questions lurking somewhere in this book, but don't cheat—see how many you can answer without looking!

1. APPROXIMATELY HOW LONG AGO DID THE BIG BANG HAPPEN?

A. 3.8 billion years ago
B. 13.8 billion years ago
C. 1.38 billion years ago

2. WHAT'S THE AVERAGE TEMPERATURE ON MARS?

A. -81.4°F (-63°C)
B. 145.4°F (63°C)
C. 1,166°F (630°C)

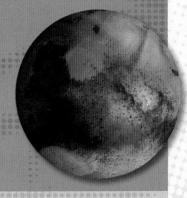

3. HOW FAR FROM EARTH IS THE VOYAGER 1 SPACECRAFT?

A. Over 124 billion mi (200 billion km)
B. Over 12.4 billion mi (20 billion km)
C. 0 km (it crashed on take off)

4. HOW MANY ASTRONAUTS HAVE WALKED ON THE MOON?

A. 10
B. 120
C. 12

5. HOW LONG DOES THE ISS TAKE TO ORBIT EARTH?
A. 90 minutes
B. 90 seconds
C. 90 days

6. IN WHICH YEAR DID NASA'S FAMOUS SPACE SHUTTLE START ITS FIRST OFFICIAL MISSION?
A. 1969
B. 2015
C. 1981

7. HOW MANY PLANETS ARE THERE IN THE SOLAR SYSTEM?
A. 4
B. 8
C. 12

8. HOW MANY TIMES WIDER IS JUPITER THAN EARTH?
A. 11 times
B. 100 times
C. 3 times

9. MERCURY IS THE FASTEST PLANET, BUT HOW FAR DOES IT TRAVEL PER SECOND?
A. 3,107 mi (5,000 km)
B. 311 mi (500 km)
C. 31 mi (50 km)

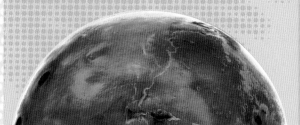

10. HOW MANY EARTHS COULD FIT IN THE SPACE BETWEEN IT AND THE MOON?
A. 30
B. 3
C. 300

Answers: 1. B. 2. A. 3. B. 4. C. 5. A. 6. C. 7. B. 8. A. 9. C. 10. A.

95

PICTURE CREDITS

The publishers would like to thank the following sources for their kind permission to reproduce the pictures in this book.

All images © Carlton Books except the following:

Page 7T: Zakharchuk/Shutterstock; 7B: structuresxx/Shutterstock; 8-9: Igor Zh./Shutterstock; 9T: NASA; 9BL: Giovanni Benintende/Shutterstock; 9BR: puchan/Shutterstock; 10: Twin Design/Shutterstock; 14C: Vadim Sadovski/Shutterstock; 14BL: AstroStar/Shutterstock; 15TR: 3Dsculptor/Shutterstock; 15R: NASA; 16T: JPL/USGS/NASA; 16BL: Johns Hopkins University Applied Physics Laboratory/Arizona State University/Carnegie Institution of Washington/NASA; 17: Johns Hopkins University Applied Physics Laboratory/Arizona State University/Carnegie Institution of Washington/NASA; 18C: NASA; 18BR: NASA; 20T: NASA; 20BC: JPL/USGS/NASA; 20BR: NASA; 21TL: NASA; 21TR: robert_s/Shutterstock; 21R: Claudio Divizia/Shutterstock; 22: robert_s/Shutterstock; 25: Merlin74/Shutterstock; 26TR: JPL/NASA; 26L: NASA; 26R: Kristina Shevchenko/Shutterstock; 27R: Jurik Peter/Shutterstock; 27B: JPL/NASA; 28C: Kristina Shevchenko/Shutterstock; 28R: Aaron Rutten/Shutterstock; 29TR: NASA; 29R: Sakdinon Kadchiangsaen/Shutterstock; 29BL: NASA; 29BR: Tristan3D/Shutterstock; 30: NASA; 31: MarcelClemens/Shutterstock; 32: NASA; 34: Dotted Yeti/Shutterstock; 35T: JPL/NASA; 35L: NASA; 36: NASA; 38: NASA; 40L: Vadim Sadovski/Shutterstock; 40C: NASA; 40BR: happydancing/Shutterstock; 41TL: NASA; 41C: NASA; 42BL: Vadim Sadovski/Shutterstock; 43: NASA; 44: Vadim Sadovski/Shutterstock; 45TL: NASA; 46: NASA; 47: AvDe/Shutterstock; 48BL: Dotted Yeti/Shutterstock; 48BR: NASA; 49TL: NASA; 49L: NASA; 49C: NASA; 49R: NASA; 49BL: NASA; 50C: JPL/USGS/NASA; 50BL: robert_s/Shutterstock; 51: puchan/Shutterstock; 52: JPL/USGS/NASA; 53T: Procy/Shutterstock; 53R: JPL/USGS/NASA; 54: mr.Timmi/Shutterstock; 56: Dabarti CGI/Shutterstock; 57L: JPL-Caltech/UCLA/MPS/DLR/IDA/NASA; 57BR: puchan/Shutterstock; 58: solarseven/Shutterstock; 59L: Myrabella/Wikimedia Commons; 59BL: NASA; 61TL: pascal/Shutterstock; 61B: ESA/Hubble/NASA; 62C: Denis Belitsky/Shutterstock; 62BL: peresanz/Shutterstock; 63BL: ESA/NASA; 63BR: vchal/Shutterstock; 64T: Wikimedia Commons; 64C: Wikimedia Commons; 64B: Wikimedia Commons; 65T: Wikimedia Commons; 65CT: Wikimedia Commons; 65CB: Wikimedia Commons; 65B: Wikimedia Commons; 66: NASA; 67TR: Vadim Sadovski/Shutterstock; 67BR: ESA/NASA; 69L: Vadim Sadovski/Shutterstock; 69BL: Nerthuz/Shutterstock; 71TR: NASA; 71R: JPL-Caltech/NASA; 72R: NASA; 72BL: 3Dsculptor/Shutterstock; 74: Andrey Armyagov/Shutterstock; 75: NASA; 76: NASA; 80: NASA; 81TC: NASA; 81TR: NASA; 81L: NASA; 81B: robert_s/Shutterstock; 83TL: NASA; 83TR: NASA; 85: NASA; 87L: Richard A McMillin/Shutterstock; 87B: 3Dstock/Shutterstock; 88C: Elenarts/Shutterstock; 88BL: Nostalgia for Infinity/Shutterstock; 88BR: sdecoret/Shutterstock; 89: NASA; 93: NASA; 94L: Igor Zh./Shutterstock; 94R: Kristina Shevchenko/Shutterstock; 95TL: NASA; 95TR: 3Dsculptor/Shutterstock; 95R: NASA; 95BL: Dotted Yeti/Shutterstock; 95BR: robert_s/Shutterstock

Every effort has been made to acknowledge correctly and contact the source and/or copyright holder of each picture and Carlton Books Limited apologizes for any unintentional errors or omissions that will be corrected in future editions of this book.